REENGINEERING FOR RESULTS

A STEP-BY-STEP GUIDE

Robert Janson   Dennis Attenello   John A. Uzzi

REENGINEERING FOR RESULTS

A STEP-BY-STEP GUIDE

Robert Janson

Dennis Attenello

John A. Uzzi

QUALITY RESOURCES®
A Division of The Kraus Organization Limited
New York, New York

Most Quality Resources books are available at quantity discounts when purchased in bulk. For more information contact:

Special Sales Department
Quality Resources
A Division of The Kraus Organization Limited
902 Broadway
New York, New York 10010
800-247-8519

Printed in the United States of America

99 98 97 96 95   10 9 8 7 6 5 4 3 2 1

Quality Resources
A Division of The Kraus Organization Limited
902 Broadway
New York, New York 10010
212-979-8600
800-247-8519

∞

The paper used in this publication meets the minimum requirements of American National Standard for Information Sciences—Permanence of Paper for Printed Library Materials, ANSI Z39.48-1984.

ISBN 0-527-76303-9

Library of Congress Cataloging-in-Publication Data

Janson, Robert.
    Reengineering for results : a step-by-step guide / Robert Janson,
  Dennis Attenello, John Uzzi.
        p.   cm.
    Includes index.
    ISBN 0-527-76303-9 (alk. paper)
    1. Reengineering (Management)   2. Organizational change-
  -Management.   3. Strategic planning.   I. Attenello, Dennis.
  II. Uzzi, John.   III. Title.
  HD58.87.J36   1995   95–19353
  658.4'06--dc20   CIP

Contents

Acknowledgments

Although there are only three authors listed on the cover of this book, the ideas expressed within resulted from collaborations with many others. The breakthrough ideas on motivation were learned from an early association with Dr. Fred Herzberg and Bob Ford. Roy W. Walters helped us understand client needs and relationships. Phil Kraft, Frank Kaveney, Ken Purdy, and Steve Carrington were our partners in learning how organizations change.

Our early research was assisted by Pat Murphy of Arthur Andersen, Tom Walther of Coopers & Lybrand, and Jewel Westerman of Travelers Insurance. Our relationship with Dr. Richard Hackman of Harvard University has always enhanced our thinking and allowed us to add academic sense to our daily consulting applications.

Some of our best collaborations have been with our clients. From those engagements, we have learned as much as we have taught. We are indebted to Ian Rolland and Dick Russell at Lincoln National Corporation for their early support of companywide change. Dick Gunderson, Chuck Dull, and Jerry Laubenstein of the Aid Association for Lutherans were fellow teammates during our process of learning how to implement self-managed teams on a large scale. Mike Magsig of Cologne Reinsurance and George Seegers of Citicorp were helpful as we thought through the various change strategies that accomplish results. Larry Buttner of First Chicago showed us how to use the early work design applications along with technology.

We would like to especially thank Clem Russo, our longtime associate who spent many hours compiling our tapes and notes.

Robert Janson
Dennis Attenello
John A. Uzzi

Preface

In only a short period of time, American businesses seem to have developed a virtual obsession with reengineering. Everywhere you look these days, there are new books, articles, and seminars that promote the benefits of this renewal strategy. And more and more companies are eagerly signing up for courses on how to tear apart their organizations and rebuild them from scratch.

But this is not a sudden development. Americans have been conducting a love affair with organizational change for some time, and there's no indication that the passion has peaked. Some experts estimate that about $50 billion will be invested in corporate change initiatives in 1995, and they expect that figure to double within a year! This is a good sign, you might think, because it demonstrates the commitment to improvement and the desire to remain economically strong and competitive.

The sad fact, however, is that Americans are often just as fickle when it comes to organizational change as in matters of the heart. In truth, we have a poor track record at remaining committed. Like the national divorce rate, the ratio between the number of improvement strategies begun and those that succeed is disheartening—and it is becoming worse. Whether it's TQM, self-managing teams, empowerment, or reengineering, many companies start out with a genuine excitement and heartfelt desire for improvement, but they repeatedly have problems staying the course or impatiently shift from one change initiative to another.

What goes wrong? The problem isn't that companies aren't sincere in their efforts, or that the strategies they try to implement aren't valuable. On the contrary, many of these initiatives are essential if organizations are to survive in the new, globally competitive environment all of us work in now. But like any good relationship, the successful marriage between an organization and the change strategy on which it relies requires perseverance, the proper skills and techniques to see it through, and sometimes even outside help.

That's why we wrote this book. We believe that reengineering offers many companies a valuable opportunity to transform themselves into more productive, more competitive, and more customer-focused organizations. But making that transition can be one of the most difficult challenges these companies ever face. To help them do it successfully, we offer our support, our advice, and our expertise in this book.

From our more than 25 years of experience in guiding organizations through large-scale change, we have developed a start-to-finish, step-by-step roadmap that companies can follow to implement their reengineering strategy. If you have decided to reengineer—or have already begun the process—we believe that you will benefit from what you read here and significantly increase the possibility that your relationship with reengineering will be a truly successful one.

Why Reengineer?
Why Now?

The president of a large corporation walks into his boardroom to address his executive team. Slowly and solemnly, he recites his predictions of the business problems he sees looming on the horizon: increased competition, smaller market share, disaffected customers, and falling profits. Then, choosing his words carefully, he recounts the strategies the company has already taken to prepare for the future and what he feels it has accomplished. "We've downsized, slashed our middle management ranks, and cut fat from every department. Yet our productivity's down, and our costs are still rising," he tells them. "We've held time-management seminars, conducted TQM training, and installed state-of-the-art technologies. And even though our people are putting in 14-hour days, our customers are still leaving us. There's only one way we can turn this situation around," he says forcefully. "Because we can't work any harder, we've got to work smarter. We've got to *reengineer!*"

How would you react if you were one of the people in that room? If you are like most of the managers and quality professionals we talk to, you would probably experience mixed emotions. Despite all the favorable press reengineering has received up to now, most business people who consider implementing it feel just as much fear as they do excitement, as much dread as optimism, as much anxiety as hope (Figure 1.1).

Even though we are advocates of the reengineering approach—and we have worked with dozens of companies to successfully manage, implement, and work through it—we understand where these business people are coming from.

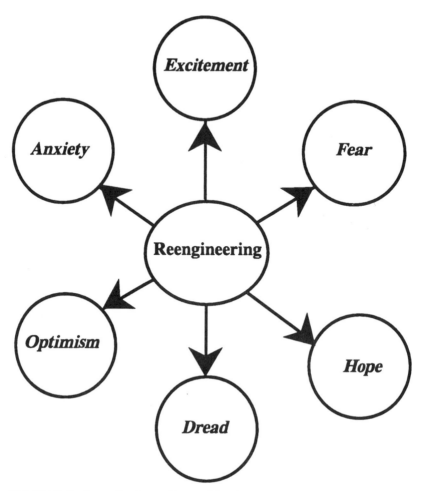

FIGURE 1.1. Feelings Caused by Reengineering

No matter how successful an improvement strategy appears to be or how many companies claim to benefit from it, it is only natural if managers are less than enthusiastic about the prospect of turning their organizations inside out, disrupting the work lives of their people, and committing themselves indefinitely to a process that promises no predictable outcome. Let's face it, reengineering entails considerable risks and a lot of hard work, and there's no guarantee that the end result will compensate for the pain endured along the way.

Yet that's not the only—perhaps not even the primary—reason many people are reluctant to embrace this radical improvement approach. Ironically, it's often those who are most accustomed to change and experimentation who are skeptical about reengineering and demonstrate the strongest resistance to it.

Their attitude: "We've tried quality circles, sociotechnical systems, participative management, work teams, and TQM, and none has delivered completely on the promises made. Now you're asking us to take what may be the biggest gamble of all: to attempt something totally new and relatively untested, that only a few large companies have achieved success with, and that potentially impacts everyone in our organization. Why should we risk everything we've accomplished so far to implement a strategy that may turn out to be just another management fad?"

For those battle-weary business people who feel that reengineering is just too new or too fashionable for them to buy in to, we always like to tell the story of the changes made in the letter-of-credit department at Citibank.

A Classic Case of Reengineering?

Citibank's letter-of-credit department is the perfect example of how traditional concepts of work efficiency helped to produce a modern-day business disaster.

Whenever a request about a letter of credit arrived at Citibank's headquarters in New York City, one of the clerks in the downstairs mail room would carefully examine the contents of the envelope and then send it along to the 24th floor. There, a small army of clerks, typists, checkers, processors, supervisors, managers, and accountants would handle the processing of this highly complex financial instrument and struggle valiantly—against somewhat staggering odds—to achieve efficiency and maintain customer satisfaction in one of Citibank's most critical operations.

First, a preprocessing clerk would determine the source of the request and direct it to the appropriate correspondent bank section within the department. Then another clerk would determine what actually had to be done as a result of the request—whether a letter of credit had to be issued, amended, or paid—with each task a clerical nightmare that tested both worker endurance and customer patience.

Merely issuing a letter of credit, for example, took an average of at least 3 days, involved more than 30 separate processing steps, and required the input of no less than 14 people. Included among them were a log-in clerk, two checkers, a central liabilities clerk, a signature control clerk, a marketing officer, and a customer service clerk. After endless hours of reading, checking, clipping, stapling, copying, verifying, and filing, the process would have to be started all over again if the customer happened to ask that the letter of credit be amended. And when the time came for payment, it took five full days before a check could be drawn up and mailed!

Citibank realized that the time-consuming and labor-intensive paper pushing that characterized this antiquated processing "system" was one reason corporate customers were giving the bank low ratings for service quality. But it also knew that installing new computers—though they might make the process more efficient—could not by themselves produce the kind of personalized service customers were now demanding. To create a department that could provide accurate, timely, and truly customized services in a variety of marketplaces, Citibank decided to redesign its entire letter-of-credit operation.

The objective was to transform the department from an assembly-line operation, in which each worker was responsible for only one function or a small piece of the work flow, into a market-focused enterprise where a single employee could service all the letter-of-credit requirements for a specific group of customers. Three major steps were involved:

1. eliminating the functional structure and reorganizing along market-segment lines

2. redesigning jobs and processes and training employees in multiple skills

3. converting from "big-box" maxicomputers to decentralized minicomputers in a distributed network

After 15 months of extensive restructuring, work redesign, and cross-training, Citibank's letter-of-credit department was still in the business of processing the financial documents that grease the wheels of international trade. But the nature of the operation had completely changed. The work that once involved bundles of cards and tickets and generated stacks of paper was now being carried out on a streamlined network of computer terminals by newly created "workstation professionals." Dedicated to specific market segments, these workers could now become intimately familiar with the needs of the customers they served and respond to them far more quickly. It now took only one employee to receive, issue, and mail out a letter of credit, and the entire transaction could be processed in less than a day (Figure 1.2).[1]

The Truth About Reengineering

The strategy Citibank used to transform its letter-of-credit department might be called a classic case of reengineering. Instead of trying to improve the sys-

KPIs	Pre-Reeng. ←——— 15 Months ———→ Post-Reeng.	
Turnaround time	72 hr min.	24 hr max.
Handoffs	14	3
Headcount	190	75
Revenue	$24M	$36M
Operating expenses	+15% per yr	No increase (5 yr)

FIGURE 1.2.   Processing Letters of Credit at Citibank

tem by making gradual or incremental changes—identifying specific problem areas and then working to make them better—Citibank chose to abandon what already existed and redesign the entire operation from start to finish. To achieve optimal organizational performance and customer satisfaction, Citibank implemented *fundamental* change in the three major aspects of its letter-of-credit business: in the way its people are organized, in how jobs are designed, and in the technology that is used to execute the work (Figure 1.3).

Yet that is not the reason why we find the Citibank case such a persuasive argument for reengineering. Many other companies have transformed themselves dramatically using this three-pronged approach, and they have achieved similarly impressive results. The General Electric Company,[2] NationsBank, The Principal Financial Group, Aid Association for Lutherans (AAL), and First National Bank of Chicago are just a few companies that have improved quality, productivity, and customer service through reengineering (Figure 1.4). What makes the Citibank case so remarkable is that it occurred almost 20 years ago!

Human Systems	+	Work Systems	+	Technological Systems	=	Successful Reengineering

FIGURE 1.3.   Components of Successful Reengineering

- Aid Association for Lutherans (AAL)

- American States

- Bankers Trust

- Citibank

- Cologne Life Reinsurance

- Fireman's Fund Insurance

- First National Bank of Chicago

- General Electric Company

- Lincoln National

- NationsBank

- New England Telephone

- The Principal Financial Group

- Union Central Life

FIGURE 1.4. Veterans of Reengineering

What that means is that reengineering is not so new or revolutionary after all. Though the name has been in use for only a few years, the principles on which reengineering is based have been around for decades. In fact, many of the changes companies make that we associate with reengineering—like re-designing simple jobs into more challenging and customer-focused ones— have an extensive history, are based on solid work theories, and represent years of organizational research and development.

Far from being a passing management fancy, reengineering is actually the culmination of a long and thorough investigation by scholars, consultants, and practitioners into how organizations can improve their operations by changing the way their people work.

The Roots of Reengineering

Where does reengineering come from? The roots of the organizational improvement strategy that we now call reengineering can be traced to a rebellion in management thinking that began more than a half-century ago. Though most managers at that time firmly adhered to the work principles laid down by Frederick Taylor, the engineer hailed as the father of "scientific management," there were some who started to question the ultimate value of Taylor's approach.

Taylor felt that the strict division of labor was the best route to efficiency and high productivity. Because the average worker could master single-task jobs faster and more thoroughly than complicated ones, he pushed for a type of work system in which jobs were broken down into their simplest components. If workers were dissatisfied because their jobs were boring and because they lacked a sense of completeness, Taylor argued, at least workers could feel a sense of pride in mastering the few simple tasks they were assigned to do.

Taylor's viewpoint was convincing and pervasive—so much so that his influence can still be seen in the production and clerical "assembly lines" that characterize many companies today. But all throughout the middle part of this century, an increasingly more vocal group of dissenting management thinkers began to chip away at Taylor's dominance.

Douglas McGregor and Frederick Herzberg were two of the most aggressive. Eventually, their work would not just "humanize" the scientific management approach, it would effectively drive a stake into the heart of the Taylor-inspired philosophy that saw mindless jobs with tight supervision as the best way to organize the way people work.[3]

From Work Motivation to Work Redesign

McGregor felt that the work system Taylor helped develop was based on a number of faulty assumptions that, collectively, he dubbed Theory X: People are basically lazy, they hate to work, and they need to be coerced and controlled in order to produce. Although Taylor's system might *make* people this way—with its emphasis on time clocks, work rules, and top–down supervision—human nature was really something quite different, McGregor claimed (Figure 1.5).

In his famous Theory Y, McGregor proposed an alternate profile of the working person: responsible, dedicated, and ingenious, with a strong potential for hard work and achievement. This theory assumed that most workers are strongly motivated *internally* and that managers need only tap into that motivation in order to improve productivity and work performance.

McGregor's theories sparked a lot of speculation over what it is that keeps workers motivated and helps them stay productive. And they prompted one distinguished psychologist, Frederick Herzberg of Case Western Reserve University, to conduct extensive research to identify these critical work "motivators." In studies with accountants and engineers in a number of large corporations, Herzberg discovered that there are many elements that do indeed contribute to keeping people happy at their jobs, including compensation systems, organizational relationships, and working conditions. But in the end, he came to the conclusion that the single most important contributor to worker motivation had nothing to do with the worker or with the organization, but with the nature of the *job itself.*

How did Herzberg know this? By asking the people who took part in his studies about the times they felt exceptionally good about their jobs and when they felt exceptionally bad, Herzberg could see that pay, benefits, company policies, work conditions, and management relations were often sources of

---

"People are not by nature passive or resistant to organizational needs. They have become so as a result of experience in organizations."

Douglas McGregor

FIGURE 1.5. McGregor's Theory of Human Nature

dissatisfaction among workers. But improving or correcting them, Herzberg discovered, did not necessarily make workers happier or more productive. By concentrating on these "satisfiers," or "hygiene" factors, as Herzberg later called them, organizations may be able to keep workers from being unhappy and head off serious unrest, but they would not be doing much to actually increase work motivation.

Surprisingly, what Herzberg found to be true job "motivators" were factors like recognition, responsibility, growth, and achievement—in other words, aspects of the work itself. These are what contribute significantly to producing long-lasting positive attitudes among workers, said Herzberg, and they should be the primary focus when an organization strives to change and improve (Figure 1.6).

How AT&T Put Herzberg to the Test

Herzberg's motivation/hygiene theory was put to the test in a series of pivotal studies conducted at AT&T in the mid-1960s. Conducted by Robert Ford, a psychologist trained at the University of Pittsburgh, this work not only confirmed Herzberg's research, it also provided specific examples of how managers could apply Herzberg's theory in their own organizations.[4]

"Satisfiers"	*"Motivators"*
• Pay	• Recognition
• Benefits	• Responsibility
• Work Conditions	• Growth
• Labor Relations	• Achievement

FIGURE 1.6. Herzberg's Motivation/Hygiene Theory

Ford had been assigned to address a significant and costly problem at AT&T: employee turnover. At that time, job opportunities were exceptionally plentiful in the United States (unemployment had hit a 15-year low of 3.3 percent!), and despite the offer of good pay, generous benefits, and excellent job security, a number of AT&T's departments and divisions were finding it increasingly difficult to keep good people.

Ford suspected that working conditions had little to do with why people were leaving the company. So taking a cue from Herzberg, he decided to focus on another possible source of the problem: work *content*. What would happen to the turnover rate at AT&T, he wondered, if the company's employees found the work that they performed intrinsically more satisfying and more rewarding?

During the next 2 years, Ford conducted a total of 19 experimental trials of "job enrichment" that involved several thousand employees throughout AT&T. And in almost every case—whether it involved service representatives, telephone operators, framemen, installers, keypunchers, or equipment engineers—Ford found that employee turnover decreased significantly when "simple" jobs were made more varied, more challenging, and more interesting (Figure 1.7).

One of the most revealing trials was conducted with groups of framemen whose job it was to connect the wires that complete new communication circuits for customers. Not only was turnover high among these groups, their work was characterized by low productivity, high error rates, and frequently missed deadlines.

Because no group of framemen really had a full work assignment, Ford felt that excessive job fragmentation was a large part of the problem. One group would write up an order, for example, a second would make the connection, and a third would test the circuit. Yet when the job was redesigned so that one team could perform all the functions from start to finish, Ford found that turnover and work errors decreased.

Another interesting trial involved a change in the responsibilities of service representatives. Although the rep's job required extensive training and was fairly complex—dealing with customers who want to order a new telephone, change service, or question a bill—most major decisions regarding the customer had to be referred to a business office supervisor.

Ford decided to introduce changes that would give some reps full responsibility for dealing with their customers. In the future, they would be able to determine credit ratings on their own, sign adjustment vouchers without management approval, and make decisions about whether to deny service for nonpayment. The organizational impact of these changes? Ford found that

- Combine into one job responsibilities that are now handled by people whose work is logically connected

- Redesign parts of the job so that employees develop stronger feelings of "my customer"

- Develop ways to give employees direct, individual feedback on their performance

- Automate routine work whenever possible

FIGURE 1.7. Ford's Guidelines for Job Enrichment

service reps who were given broader responsibilities were not only less likely to leave AT&T, they also made fewer mistakes in their work, provided faster service, and demonstrated more positive service attitudes.

The Legacy of Herzberg and Ford

Ford's attempts to validate Herzberg's motivation/hygiene theory were a critical breakthrough in understanding the strong relationship between job satisfaction and organizational performance. And by focusing on how to bring about change through the redesign of work, they planted the seeds of the movement that would later grow into reengineering.

Herzberg and Ford also provided many business practitioners—especially change agents like us—with a firm theoretical foundation we could build on to develop effective strategies for organizational improvement.

On the Road to Reengineering

It took almost three decades for the pioneering work of Herzberg and Ford to develop into the change strategy we now know as reengineering. But the evolution from one to the other is indisputable, and much of it can be traced through our experience.

Almost all of our early work revolved around the revolutionary ideas of Herzberg and Ford. Our company's founding members, in fact, participated as AT&T line managers in the mid-1960s and were on the team charged with evaluating Ford's job-enrichment studies. This experience led to our development of a practical instrument companies could use to implement Ford's job redesign approach—the Work Effectiveness Model.

Developing a Blueprint for Management Action

The Work Effectiveness Model was developed from research we conducted in a number of organizations, including The Travelers Insurance Companies, with behavioral scientists J. Richard Hackman of Yale and Greg Oldham of the University of Illinois. For the first time, it established a set of tools managers could use to *diagnose* the motivational level of existing jobs, and it provided a blueprint for translating those results into specific action steps for change (Figure 1.8).[5]

How did the model work? Following on the heels of Herzberg and his followers, the model started by reaffirming the three "psychological states" that they said were critical in determining a worker's job satisfaction:

- *experienced meaningfulness* (the degree to which the worker finds the job worthwhile or important)

- *experienced responsibility* (the degree to which the worker feels personally accountable for job results)

- *knowledge of results* (the degree to which the worker can determine whether job performance is satisfactory)

Then, drawing from our own research, the model identified five "core job dimensions" that we found to be key to creating and maintaining these three psychological states:

1. *skill variety* (the degree to which a job challenges the worker's skills and abilities)

2. *task identity* (the degree to which the job completes a "whole" or identifiable piece of work)

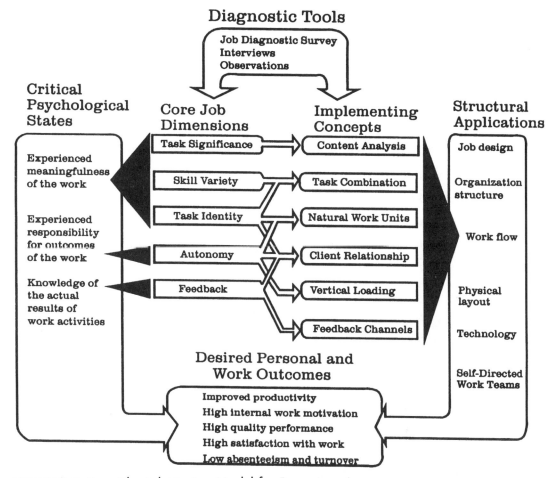

FIGURE 1.8. The Job Design Model for Reengineering

3. *task significance* (the degree to which the job has a substantial and perceivable impact on others)

4. *autonomy* (the degree to which the job gives the worker freedom, independence, and discretion in determining how to carry out the work)

5. *feedback* (the degree to which the worker receives information about his or her performance)

Finally, the model outlined six basic action strategies for changing jobs so workers would remain motivated and productive. These strategies, which we called "implementing concepts," included:

1. *content analysis* (identifying and eliminating unnecessary work)

2. *task combination* (redesigning fragmented jobs so that all the tasks required to process a given piece of work are performed by one individual)

3. *natural work units* (batching together into one job all the tasks that relate to a single product or customer)

4. *client relationships* (establishing direct contact with customers—either internal or external)

5. *vertical loading* (pushing responsibilities down from higher supervisory levels)

6. *feedback channels* (giving workers immediate information about their performance)

Measuring the Impact of Work Effectiveness

The Work Effectiveness Model helped to validate Herzberg's theory and Ford's experiments, and it became integral to the job-enrichment approach that dominated work redesign in the 1970s. Even college professors began to integrate the model into their courses on organizational psychology and development. Its internal logic and consistency may have been one reason why it was so popular. But we believe there was a much simpler explanation behind the model's appeal: It worked!

In the dozens of companies that in those days were looking to improve morale and employee well-being, the application of the Work Effectiveness Model consistently resulted in increased motivation and greater job satisfaction. What's more, whenever these companies redesigned jobs so that workers had more control over what they did, felt a greater sense of job ownership, and were more challenged each day, there were other, no less significant, organizational outcomes: noticeable improvements in product or service quality and productivity.

For example, with keypunch operators in one department at The Travelers we noticed that those whose jobs were redesigned scored higher in surveys measuring job satisfaction, and their rate of absenteeism—another important gauge of employee morale—dropped by almost 25 percent. Yet these workers had changed in other important ways, too. A comparison of statistics collected before and after the study showed that they had become almost 40 percent more productive and that their collective error rate had dropped by over a third. As a result of job redesign, the company calculated, The Travelers was saving almost $100,000 a year in this department alone (Figure 1.9).

Over the coming years, it was the growing need for improvements in these areas—quality, productivity, and cost efficiency—that became the primary reason many companies became so interested in the job-enrichment approach. And they began to ask us to implement it on a much broader scale. By the late 1970s, we began hearing from presidents and CEOs—not just directors of human resources—and we were no longer working just in single departments or individual business units, but had begun to introduce work redesign strategies companywide.

From Work Effectiveness to Reengineering

It's important to remember that the reengineering approach we now practice—and describe in this book—is something we adopted gradually, after many years of trial and experimentation.

When the Work Effectiveness Model was implemented throughout entire companies, for example, it became apparent that the benefits of job redesign increased significantly when the approach was extended beyond a single department or function. But over the years, another interesting phenomenon

---

- Random batch assignments were eliminated and each worker was assigned continuing responsibility for specific accounts.

- Operators, not their supervisors, were to inspect documents for accuracy and legibility and take up problems directly with clients.

- Incorrect cards would be returned for revisions to the operator who punched them.

- Operators were given the authority to set their own schedules and plan their daily work.

FIGURE 1.9.   Implementing Work Effectiveness Concepts at The Travelers

was observed: In those companies that complemented these work redesign changes with more extensive training, new recognition and reward systems, more participative management styles, and more innovative uses of technology, improvements in quality, productivity, and efficiency often registered statistical quantum leaps. Instead of rising by 20 or 30 percent, productivity would double; instead of falling by a third, error rates would tumble to practically nothing.

This was borne out in the mid-1980s with the Aid Association for Lutherans (AAL), where 17 multiskilled teams were created in the company's Insurance Product Services department, with each team performing all the 167 tasks that had formerly been split along functional lines. These work redesign changes alone would have helped improve productivity. But when combined with other major changes the company made—including new computer systems, training for team members in self-management, and a reorganization along product lines—the final results were far more impressive: case-processing time, for example, was reduced by 75 percent! In the end, AAL became a company that not only worked better, but one that had gained considerable competitive advantage in its industry (Figure 1.10).[6]

Just like Citibank a decade before, AAL used a three-pronged change strategy (*human* system + *work* system + *technology* system) that would today be classified as reengineering. Although the term was not in use then, the reengineering formula existed and had been applied effectively in a number of companies, including First National Bank of Chicago, Fidelity Union Life, and Crown Life Insurance Company. By the time reengineering was "born"

- Case processing time reduced by 75 percent

- Supervisory positions reduced from 62 to 22

- Over 50 full-time positions eliminated, with savings of $1 million

- Improved relations between home office and field agencies

FIGURE 1.10. Reengineering Results at AAL

in the early 1990s, in fact, it had already enjoyed a long and successful history in America's business community.

Reengineering Then and Now

The fundamental work redesign principles that comprise the heart and soul of reengineering have changed little in the 20 years since the development of the Work Effectiveness Model. But the business world in which we now apply these principles is dramatically different. Increased competition, shrinking markets, and rapidly rising consumer expectations have created a more volatile and unpredictable economic climate. And that's forcing many companies to shed their old organizational forms—multilayered, highly functionalized, and culturally bureaucratic—in order to become leaner, more flexible, and more responsive to their customers.

As a result, more companies are asking for help to reengineer than ever before. But it's not just because they want to; it's because they *have* to. They realize that only reengineering can bring about the kinds of comprehensive and fundamental changes that they must make today. And only through reengineering can they achieve the breakthrough improvements in quality, productivity, and customer satisfaction that will help them to survive and prosper in today's competitive marketplace.

The speed with which reengineering can make a difference is another factor that explains its current popularity. Unlike TQM and other improvement strategies that are based on the slow accumulation of incremental changes, reengineering produces results quickly—in 12 to 18 months in most cases—and has a bottom-line impact almost immediately. This appeals to many American companies that suddenly find themselves in the position of playing "catch-up." They can't afford to wait years for the kinds of business results they need to keep pace with their competitors—or to push ahead of them.

For them and for many other American companies, the critical question these days is not why reengineer, but when.

The Shifting Focus of Reengineering

The reengineering approach that we practice today, then, is the product of two converging historical forces: a long and solid tradition of motivation theory and work redesign, and the unique business pressures that are now bearing down on American companies. You might even say that reengineering was a solution waiting for a problem to happen, and it did not have to wait very long.

Those companies that used reengineering in its earliest forms were addressing real problems, too, though they were markedly different from the issues businesses focus on today. Back then, companies that "reengineered" were concerned primarily with improving the morale and well-being of their workers. Their motives were not altogether altruistic—they were well aware of the organizational benefits of increased job satisfaction. But the change strategies they employed were essentially *worker*-driven.

In most cases today, however, reengineering is a *customer*-driven change process. True, it still results in jobs that are more satisfying and more challenging, and work redesign is still a primary component of the reengineering equation. But the overall success of reengineering in any company today must be gauged by the impact it has on that company's customers. After all, in the highly competitive environment we work in today, winning new customers and building the strong and lasting relationships that help keep them is the business game that we are all required to play.

This shift in focus does not alter the validity of the work design principles on which reengineering is based. But it may have an impact on the objectives of an organization's change process or on its scope. When companies today make decisions about which jobs to change and how to change them, for example, they first take into account what their customers are looking for and what they need most. Employee satisfaction remains an important reengineering goal, but satisfying customers has become the overriding consideration when designing more effective work processes and more rewarding and challenging jobs.

As a customer-driven process, reengineering also tends to become a bigger change effort and to involve more aspects of the organization that undertakes it. Improvement efforts that are worker-driven need only concern themselves directly with how jobs are designed and how they are carried out. But change that is customer-driven must often cast a wider net and seek opportunities for improvement companywide.

Five Reengineering Myths

The purpose in relating the rich history of work redesign in this chapter is to provide some reassurance to those managers who are considering reengineering and to help them feel more confident about implementing it. Negative myths about reengineering, however, continue to proliferate and many managers still have their doubts and reservations.

We hope we can remove most of those doubts in the coming chapters as we present our step-by-step guide. But before the details of implementation are discussed, we would like to state our position up front on some of the other controversial beliefs surrounding this important change strategy:

Reengineering can be implemented effectively only in large companies.
True, most articles on reengineering and seminars that promote it spotlight large and well-known American corporations such as Taco Bell, Hallmark, Whirlpool, and Bell Atlantic. But over the past decade, many small and mid-size companies have successfully implemented the reengineering approach. In the coming chapters, we will describe some of those applications, and show how reengineering has helped these companies become better competitors in their own markets and industries.

Reengineering always requires major investments in new technologies.
Advanced technology is one of the tools that companies often rely on when they reengineer, but large systems changes are not always necessary. Many companies make significant progress in productivity, quality improvement, and customer service strictly through a more creative use of personal computers and local-area networks. We will even describe how one organization was able to double its productivity and reduce operating expenses without introducing any new technologies at all!

Reengineering has a high failure rate. Some management experts claim that reengineering is so difficult that most of the companies that attempt to implement it fail to do it successfully. We could not disagree more. As you will learn, reengineering is a process many organizations can benefit from. Results will vary from company to company, of course. But our experience has shown that virtually every organization that makes the commitment to learn and apply reengineering concepts and tools can improve significantly.

Reengineering means downsizing. Many recent success stories of companies that have reengineered emphasize the productivity and cost benefits that result from organizational change, reinforcing the notion that reengineering means to cut jobs and reduce head count. Experience shows, however, that the best reengineering efforts establish multiple success targets—improved profitability, increased customer satisfaction, and more meaningful jobs—and that organizational change with a one-note focus is likely to produce far less significant results.

Reengineering means destroying your organization and rebuilding it from scratch. Some managers fear that reengineering will be too disruptive—perhaps even devastating—to their company, and others believe that it's an uncontrollable process: Once you start it, you never really know where you might end up. There's also the widespread anxiety of throwing the baby out with the bathwater. In order to "reinvent" your organization, some managers think, you have to be willing to sacrifice everything that's good about it, too.

These fears are based on a misunderstanding of how reengineering works. While it's true that reengineering always involves fundamental change, that's often achieved by modifying or improving what already exists—not necessarily by eliminating it. And even when radical measures are required, their impact can be predicted and even planned. Like demolition experts who blow up buildings in crowded inner cities—bringing down major structures in a controlled and precise manner—managers can make important changes in their organizations with minimal damage and disruption by following a well-orchestrated reengineering process.

In the following chapters, we will describe that process to you in detail and show how you can implement it with success.

Notes

1. For a more detailed description of how Citibank reengineered its letter-of-credit department, see Richard J. Matteis, "The New Back Office Focuses on Customer Service," *Harvard Business Review* (March-April 1979): pp. 146–159.

2. See Robert Frigo and Robert Janson, "GE's Financial Services Operation Achieves Quality Results Through 'Work-Out' Process," *National Productivity Review* (Winter 1993/94): pp. 53–61.

3. An excellent history of job redesign and organizational development is included in Marvin Weisbord, *Productive Workplaces: Organizing and Managing for Dignity, Meaning, and Community* (San Francisco: Jossey-Bass, 1987).

4. For a description of Ford's studies at AT&T, see Robert N. Ford, *Motivation Through the Work Itself* (New York: AMACOM, 1969).

5. See J. Richard Hackman, Greg Oldham, Robert Janson, and Kenneth Purdy, "A New Strategy For Job Enrichment," *California Management Review* (Summer 1975): pp. 57–71.

6. For more information on AAL's change strategy, see Robert Janson and Richard L. Gunderson, "The Team Approach to Companywide Change," *National Productivity Review* (Winter 1990/91): pp. 35–44.

2

Taking the Plunge: Making the Decision to Reengineer

Several years ago, we met with an executive vice president of a major insurance company, which we felt was a strong candidate for reengineering. There were several organizational symptoms that led us to this evaluation: a growing expense gap caused by rapidly rising costs, a highly functionalized structure with narrowly defined jobs, and a corporate culture that was slow to innovate. Though the company had a good reputation and a strong financial history, it was clear that major changes had to be made if it was going to maintain its leading position in an industry becoming increasingly more competitive and service oriented.

Several weeks later this executive called us up with what he called "both good news and bad news." "The good news," he reported, "is that you've convinced me that reengineering major segments of my organization could help us become more efficient and responsive to customers. It's strong medicine, but I really believe that it could ensure this company's future. But," he added, "the bad news is I still haven't decided whether or not to do it."

Undoubtedly, there are those who would interpret this executive's indecisiveness as a lack of courage or a sign of management weakness. However, there was wisdom in his hesitation. Instinctively, he knew that in order to succeed at a major change effort like reengineering, it wasn't enough that his organization had a *need* to reengineer. It also had to be *ready* to reengineer. And that was a determination he felt would take more time to make.

All too often, executives make the decision to reengineer in desperation or in haste. Like the fictitious company president introduced at the beginning of

Chapter 1, many executives turn to reengineering as a last resort or a "magic pill" they believe will cure all their business problems. Or because of its current popularity, they see reengineering as the only change strategy that will give them significant results today.

What these executives fail to realize, however, is that reengineering is not appropriate for every business situation. Though we firmly believe in the merits of reengineering, there are companies—especially those operating in a firefighting or crisis mode—that are simply not strong or stable enough to undertake such radical change. These companies should put out all their fires before they reengineer, or they should consider implementing another change strategy: Though it may be less comprehensive than reengineering, it would also be less demanding.

Business Strategy Comes First

In our experience, few executives ever regret their decision to reengineer. But an important part of their success is the work they perform up front to make sure that certain prerequisites have been met before the change process begins.

One of the most important elements to any large-scale change effort like reengineering is a clearly formulated and workable business strategy. Reengineering can't rescue a company that's working from a bad business plan, nor should it ever be seen as a substitute for strategy. Companies should not reengineer if they do not know where they are going, who their customers are, or what markets they are competing in. Those that do often find themselves building skyscrapers on sand: redesigning the wrong work processes, for example, or trying to improve a business that may no longer be salvageable.

For one midsize health insurance carrier that failed to heed this warning, the consequences were disastrous. Like others in its industry, this company faced a volatile and unpredictable marketplace and constant regulatory changes. Yet even though it couldn't see around the next corner, it made the decision to reengineer and frantically began to restructure itself and redesign core business processes at full speed. Much of this work had to be undone at great expense when the company repositioned to service a new market niche and began to move in a different strategic direction.

The Spectrum of Corporate Change

Besides the lack of a solid strategic foundation, there are other reasons why a company should decide not to reengineer: It may need to concentrate its en-

- You're operating in a crisis mode.

- You don't have a clearly formulated business strategy.

- You need to focus on developing new products or penetrating new markets.

- You're struggling to establish internal stability.

- You're looking for a "magic pill" to solve all your business problems.

FIGURE 2.1.   Do NOT Reengineer If...

ergies on developing a new product or penetrating new markets, for example, or it may have to reestablish internal stability after a recent acquisition or merger (Figure 2.1). That does not mean that other steps can't be taken to help the company change and improve, however. Making the decision to reengineer should never be seen as an either/or choice: Either you reengineer or you do nothing.

Unfortunately, this mind-set is all too pervasive in the business world today. As market conditions become increasingly more difficult, many executives feel that they have to do *something* to help their companies compete. And based on what they read in newspapers and business journals, reengineering seems to be the only game in town.

But corporate change and improvement should be viewed as a spectrum of activities that you can choose from, and the strategy you decide to go with should depend on both the scope and depth of the changes you want to achieve (Figure 2.2).

On one end of the corporate change spectrum are those strategies that focus on one or only a few work processes, or that rely on continuous, incremental improvement. These strategies often consist of project-oriented, bottom–up initiatives that will help you to stretch your existing targets or fine-tune work processes that are already in place. Although it is unlikely that these strategies will convert you from an industry laggard into a global leader, they may be effective if you want to do the following:

What to change	Single function	Single work process	Multiple work processes	Integrated business units
How to change	Quality teams/task force	Cross-functional team	Cross-functional teams	Business redesign
Change objective	Incremental improvement	Radical improvement	Organizational transformation	Strategic realignment

FIGURE 2.2. The Spectrum of Corporate Change

- bridge gaps with benchmarking partners or competitors
- align work processes more closely with established organizational objectives
- work solely on improving a critical department or function

Large-scale change efforts like reengineering fall on the farthest end of the corporate change spectrum. They give you the most significant results, of course, but they are also the most radical options you can choose and the ones that require the most time, planning, and resources. Change strategies like reengineering are appropriate for the following:

- if you want to achieve dramatic improvements in quality, productivity, and service
- if the scope of your work redesign efforts crosses many functional boundaries and organizational levels
- if the strategic or cultural impact you are striving for is so great that the change effort requires leadership from the topmost levels of your company.

Three Critical Questions

Improvement strategies like reengineering comprise only part of the corporate change spectrum, although they are the ones that will give you the greatest payback. Why would any corporate leader choose a strategy less ambitious? Because the decision to reengineer should not be based on need or desire alone. As we stated before, other factors must also be taken into account: your organization's readiness for change, for example, and its willingness to undertake a long and difficult change process. That's why you should always ask yourself these three critical questions before you commit to the reengineering approach:

1. Do you need to reengineer?

2. Are you ready to reengineer?

3. Do you know what you're getting yourself into?

Do You Need to Reengineer?

There are basically three corporate situations where reengineering can address a real business need (Figure 2.3). The first is when you face or anticipate major problems—you are losing market share in a thriving industry, for example, or rising costs are draining your profits—and you need to take immediate corrective action (the *troubleshooter*). The second situation is when you anticipate a major change in the marketplace you serve or in the technology you use, and you want to make sure that you don't fall behind your competition (the *early adapter*). The third situation is when you want to leapfrog all the others in your industry to establish your company as a trendsetter or market leader (the *first mover*).

• *Troubleshooters*	Do you need to solve a serious internal or external problem?
• *Early adapters*	Do you need to move faster to keep up with changes in your industry?
• *First movers*	Do you want to leapfrog your competition and become a global leader?

FIGURE 2.3.   Reengineering Candidates

Troubleshooters. Companies that are experiencing internal or external difficulties are often good candidates for reengineering. Escalating expenses, high turnover, or falling profits are all problems that reengineering can address and reverse, as are external indicators of distress, such as increased customer complaints and falling market share.

The Individual Insurance operation of The Principal Financial Group and AAL's Insurance Products Services division are two organizations that qualified as "troubleshooters." Although each organization was growing and financially sound before it reengineered, expenses were rising faster than revenues in both cases, and that was a major factor contributing to their decision to change.

Early adapters. A company's desire to keep pace with current market trends—or to get a head start on future ones—is also a good reason to reengineer. Early adapters may not have to change now, but they know that change is inevitable sooner or later and that it is better to avert a crisis than have to respond to it unprepared.

The First National Bank of Chicago qualified as an early adapter because it made the decision to reengineer its Commercial Loan Operations Division based on new trends it discovered in customer expectations. Although the bank's service ratings were relatively high for its industry, First Chicago knew that it had to change the highly fragmented work processes that characterized its commercial lending function in order to provide business customers with the flexible, accurate, and speedy service that more and more of them were beginning to demand.

First movers. Companies that strive to be the best in their field or who want to be recognized as world leaders in service, technology, or quality may also feel a need to reengineer. Like Disney, Hallmark, Maytag, Federal Express, and GE,[1] these companies refuse to rest on their laurels and work continuously to improve what they offer so that they always stand out from the rest of the pack.

One CEO in the entertainment industry, for example, initiated a reengineering effort after three consecutive years of record revenues and profits. The motivation behind this decision? Given the fickle nature of his market and the volatility of his business, he knew that he constantly had to redefine the product his company offered if it was to remain on top, and reengineering is one way to instill that culture of constant change and improvement.

The Reengineering Smell Test

By establishing these three categories, we do not mean to imply that all companies that reengineer fall within one or the other (all three categories may apply at once, for example), or that the need for reengineering can always be determined objectively. In many cases, in fact, making the decision to reengineer is a highly subjective and intuitive act that's based on a general feeling—usually the president's or CEO's—that the organization is not performing as well as it could and that it's ripe for radical change.

New chief executives often reengineer because they come in to their organization with a fresh perspective. Not having contributed to the existing situation, they can more easily see the potential within their company and envision the impact that a major change effort can have. This was the case at AAL, where a new president took charge in 1986 and immediately began a series of in-depth interviews with the company's 100 top executives. His suspicions were confirmed that organizational change was needed. (In the end, this proved to be a smart move for several reasons: It not only helped the president to formulate a preliminary change agenda, it also gave him the opportunity to become familiar with the management talent he was working with and to build a strong political base in support of renewal.)

Long-standing presidents and CEOs can also conduct informal talks with customers, other managers, and employees at all levels about how the organization is doing, how it can improve, and what its prospects are for the future. In this way, they usually gain a new assessment of their organization and develop a better understanding of where and how much it needs to change.

Another way to gauge the need to reengineer that any manager can do is to staple yourself, figuratively speaking, to a typical order form to find out what your customers go through in buying your product or service. Or simply follow the steps your customers take when interacting with the people in your organization. This will give you a good sense of which jobs or work activities add value for customers, which should be redesigned or eliminated, and how extensive an overhaul is necessary.

Reengineering Self-Test

In many cases, only by conducting "walk-through" exercises like these can you learn what you have to know in order to decide whether your company needs to reengineer (Figure 2.4). Together with a strong knowledge of business

- Does your organization have to make quantum leaps in productivity or quality?

- Will new technologies require major changes in how you work?

- Do you have the infrastructure to support high-involvement teams?

- Do you need to totally transform yourself to meet your challenges?

FIGURE 2.4.   Reasons for Reengineering

conditions and market trends, the deeper understanding you gain of how your organization operates is essential in answering the kinds of questions that are critical in this decision-making process:

- *Does your organization have to make quantum leaps (30, 40, 50 percent, or more) in reducing your costs, improving productivity and quality, or cutting turnaround times?* If your research shows that expenses are rising faster than your revenues, or that there's a significant gap between what your customers expect and what your people deliver, then you may need to reengineer.

- *Are new technologies available (or on the way) that will require major changes in the way you work or in your culture?* If your research indicates that your people are not prepared to adapt smoothly and quickly to a new technology that's essential to your business, then you may need to reengineer.

- *If you intend to move to high-involvement teams, do you have the infrastructure to support them?* If you suspect that your organization may not be able to successfully make the transition to more participative work structures, then you may need to reengineer.

- *Does your organization need to revitalize itself to meet the business challenges of the next decade?* If you feel that nothing short of a total transformation is necessary to help your organization keep pace with changing market conditions and new customer expectations, then you may need to reengineer.

For those who answer no to all these questions, a change strategy other than reengineering may be able to take them where they want to go. But those who answer yes probably will not be satisfied with the results they achieve from less radical change strategies, like continuous improvement or TQM. These people may have a real need to reengineer, and they should address the second critical question in deciding whether or not to take this important organizational step.

Are You Ready to Reengineer?

Reengineering is never implemented without difficulty, but some companies are more prepared for it than others and move through the process faster and more easily. Those that have already decentralized much of their information and decision making, for example, introduced high-performance work teams, or pushed accountability down to fairly low levels may be better able to absorb major changes and find the rigors of reengineering less demanding.

This is not to say that companies unfamiliar with change should avoid the reengineering approach. In many cases, these are the organizations that need to reengineer the most, though they may have to go through a period of psychological and cultural preparation before they start. One large insurance company, for example, decided to move to self-directed work teams after decades of operating in a highly functional, paternalistic, and hierarchical manner. Eventually, the company made the crossover to teams with spectacular results, but it had to spend an entire year acclimating its people by implementing transitional teams, conducting communication skills workshops, and constantly heralding the benefits of increased participation.

Companies operating in a crisis mode should also postpone reengineering until they have achieved at least a modicum of organizational stability. That way they will not be sidetracked from the improvement process and will be better able to handle significant change without undue distress.

One large bank whose business operations were in a state of total chaos had to use this advice—mortgage applications were backlogged, phones were left unanswered, and service levels were substandard. The company's executives initiated some change efforts that were functionally focused (restricted to specific departments or functions) and control-oriented (mandated from above, without seeking participation or input from others). Those weren't the characteristics they were looking for in the type of company they hoped to eventually become, but they knew they had to do a better job of managing their day-to-day business before they could begin to reengineer.

Analyzing Preexisting Conditions

There are several important factors that should be taken into consideration when analyzing your organization's readiness for reengineering (Figure 2.5):

Previous change experience. Your past experience with change is usually a good indicator of how well you will succeed with reengineering. If you have a strong tradition of organizational improvement, if better quality and increased productivity are established company priorities, and if your company understands that change is an essential component of business success today, then you and your organization may be ready to reengineer.

Proceed with caution, however, if reengineering would come at the end of a long series of frustrating and unsuccessful change efforts. Too many improvement programs can breed skepticism, indifference, and an attitude that "this too shall pass." So before implementing another major change effort, you may have to invest time and energy building credibility—at least until you can regenerate the kind of energy and enthusiasm that reengineering requires.

• *Previous change experience*	Do you have the energy and enthusiasm to undertake another improvement effort?
• *Levels of resistance*	Is there a strong sense of teamwork and a willingness to cooperate?
• *Manpower requirements*	Do your managers have the loyalty and confidence of their people?
• *Management priorities*	Can you devote enough time and energy to reengineering?
• *Organizational resolve*	Do you have the courage it takes to change and improve?

FIGURE 2.5.   Are You Ready for Reengineering?

Levels of resistance. Change is always difficult and sometimes threatening for people, so it's only natural that some resistance will be encountered when it is introduced. But in most cases, normal levels of resistance will not undermine the attempts to reengineer, and resistance is often diminished or overcome as the reengineering effort proceeds.

If you have just come out of a poorly managed merger, however, or if your company has recently conducted a series of major layoffs, then resistance levels may be too high and the time may not be right to reengineer. In order to succeed, any major change effort requires a strong sense of teamwork and a willingness to cooperate, and those may be lacking if labor–management relations are badly strained, for example, or if the work force is feeling significantly threatened or insecure.

Manpower requirements. The most successful reengineering efforts are those that are characterized by strong leadership from the top, and that comes only from managers who are experienced, knowledgeable, and dedicated to the success of their organization. Like other change strategies, reengineering always involves participation of the rank and file, but management's contribution is also critical in reengineering because the process is more comprehensive and entails more risk.

Do not try to reengineer if your senior management staff is unwilling or unable to invest its time and energy in the process or if your middle management ranks have recently been decimated through downsizing. Our advice: Before undertaking a significant change effort like reengineering, make sure there is a core group of managers who are committed to seeing the process through, who understand thoroughly how the business operates, and who have the loyalty and confidence of their people.

Management priorities. For reengineering to achieve the best results, it must be made a top organizational priority. Companies that are considering reengineering but are preoccupied with opening new markets, introducing new computer systems, or cutting costs through downsizing would do better to postpone the implementation of their change effort until they can give it the attention required.

Senior executives in charge of a reengineering effort must be willing to devote most of their time and energy to it. When reengineering is conducted organizationwide, the CEO or president always takes a lead role, but because of the complexities of change, some companies create another high-profile position—sometimes called the "chief change officer" (CCO)—who holds the primary responsibility for coordinating multiple initiatives across departments or units, communicating goals and objectives, and tracking results over time.

Organizational resolve. Reengineering can be difficult and frustrating, and progress is sometimes interspersed with failures and setbacks. So unless your organization can boast of substantial reserves of courage, patience, and perseverance, it's unlikely that you will be able to see this challenging process through to the end.

For that reason, the reengineering approach is not recommended for organizations that are racked by labor–management strife, where morale has been seriously weakened by repeated layoffs, or where a recent merger or acquisition has impaired organizational unity and cohesion. In those cases, it's often best to take steps first to improve the psychological well-being of the organization—and give people time to regain their ability to cope with change and uncertainty—before embarking on the reengineering journey.

The Prerequisites of Reengineering

If you feel that your company has a strong need to reengineer you should not delude yourself into thinking that your desire for change will compensate for your lack of readiness. Although reengineering can help companies become more efficient, improve quality, and serve their customers better, it isn't a magic remedy for every business problem—and the results it achieves can be quickly undone when organizations attempt it prematurely. To work best, reengineering requires a certain degree of organizational health and stability and the basic resources needed to undertake major change.

If you feel that your company meets these prerequisites you should then consider the final question in the reengineering decision-making process.

Do You Know What You're Getting Yourself Into?

Understandably, those who reengineer have high expectations. When they make the decision to go through a difficult and prolonged period of restructuring and work redesign, they believe they will reap significant benefits in organizational efficiency, work productivity, and service quality. In the vast majority of cases, these expectations are either met or exceeded. But many times reengineering also brings about results that were not anticipated—shifts in political power, for example, sudden and unanticipated resistance to the change effort, or challenges to management authority (Figure 2.6).

Why does this happen? In the process of transforming into a future and more desirable state, every organization that reengineers must pass through a state of flux and transition, and what happens in that intermediate state cannot always be predicted. Though it's tempting to think of your organization as a large machine where parts can be changed precisely and exactly as planned, the reality is altogether different. Changes made in one part of your organization may spill over into another, they may be highly disruptive to day-to-day operations, or they may have broad cultural ramifications that can't always be foreseen or controlled.

Reengineering is more comprehensive and more radical than any other change strategy you may have used or contemplated—and as a consequence, it entails more risks. So when your company makes the decision to reengineer, you must be aware of what's likely to happen and be willing to confront and work through these eventualities. There are four that typically catch executives by surprise when their companies reengineer.

Loss of control. Because of its scope, reengineering always requires strong leadership from the top, but participation is also essential to making it work. For managers at all levels, that means surrendering some authority and decision-making power to their subordinates—at least during the transition period, and sometimes for good.

• *Loss of control*	Are you prepared for the permanent cultural changes that reengineering may produce?
• *Shifting balance of power*	Can you maintain political stability during periods of turbulence and uncertainty?
• *Noncompliance*	Do you have a plan to win over those who oppose the change effort?

FIGURE 2.6. Results of Reengineering That May Not Be Anticipated

Like other major improvement strategies, reengineering works best when employees are involved in its planning and execution—in data collection, problem diagnosis, new concept development, and change implementation. (At AAL, for example, some of the most dramatic results achieved were conceived and carried out by teams of workers at the lowest levels of the organization.) But it's important to remember that once the participative mind-set takes root, it's difficult to revert to more traditional ways of operating. In opening new doors, reengineering often produces significant and sometimes permanent cultural changes that everyone should be aware of and be prepared for.

Shifting balance of power. Any major change effort creates anxiety, uncertainty, and confusion, and that often has an impact on an organization's political dynamics. When people feel insecure, they are more likely to engage in activities that will influence, obstruct, or undermine others, or they may group together to establish new centers of power to assure themselves a solid position in the emerging organization. Whereas some shifts in political power are a healthy response to the extensive changes brought about by reengineering, major power struggles can seriously disrupt the improvement process, create a dysfunctional operation, and divert attention from more important goals and objectives.

What can be done to promote political stability during periods of change and transition? One way is to appoint a transition manager—usually a high-level executive who is well known in the company—who has the power and authority to manage the change process and commands the respect of different power groups within the organization. Another way is to establish a transition management structure—a reengineering steering team or special task force, for example. That often provides an organizational "anchor" during periods of turbulence and helps allay the feelings that lead to defensive behaviors.

Insubordination or noncompliance. Almost every reengineering effort provokes resistance from those who have a vested interest in maintaining the status quo. But you may also face problems from those who oppose change on business or ideological grounds: They may not agree with your analysis of market trends, for example, or they may truly believe that the current way of operating is better than whatever reengineering can achieve. No matter what their reason is, these people often feel justified in deploying obstructionist tactics and sometimes encourage noncompliance with reengineering goals.

One way to neutralize potential insurgents is to win over key managers and power groups in order to build a critical mass in support of change. When change is championed by those who have the respect and loyalty of their people, it's much easier to convince naysayers of the benefits of reengineering and to generate the kind of energy needed for organizational renewal. Another strategy for converting change opponents: Modify your incentive systems to acknowledge and reward those who commit themselves to the reengineering effort and who work vigorously to make it a success.

Transitional roles. Reengineering is never accomplished without a significant increase in organizational stress. Employees must often learn new and more complicated jobs, undergo extensive training, and adjust to more collaborative work styles. And these challenges can cause increased anxiety and feelings of inadequacy. During the transition period, many come to rely more heavily on the people they report to for comfort, moral support, and information—and managers suddenly find themselves thrust into a new role: change agent.

All managers who reengineer must take on new responsibilities in helping their people to cope with major change and make it through the transition. Among their most important duties are the following:

- clearly communicate the goals and purposes of reengineering

- work closely with those who find it difficult to disengage from the present state

- build in effective mechanisms that provide feedback and encouragement

- share information regularly about the progress of the change effort and about problems that must be overcome

- model the new behaviors needed to make reengineering succeed

Choosing Reengineering

Some companies reengineer because they feel that they have no other options, and their change efforts are often characterized by the reluctance and lack of enthusiasm that accompanied their reengineering decision. But companies that truly choose reengineering usually fare much better. They reengineer because they *want* to: They know they have a need to do it; they feel ready for it; and they go into the process with their eyes wide open. In most cases, these companies achieve better results, and they are far more successful at introducing permanent and lasting change (Figure 2.7).

In the next chapter, we will discuss how you can prepare your organization once the important decision to reengineer has been made.

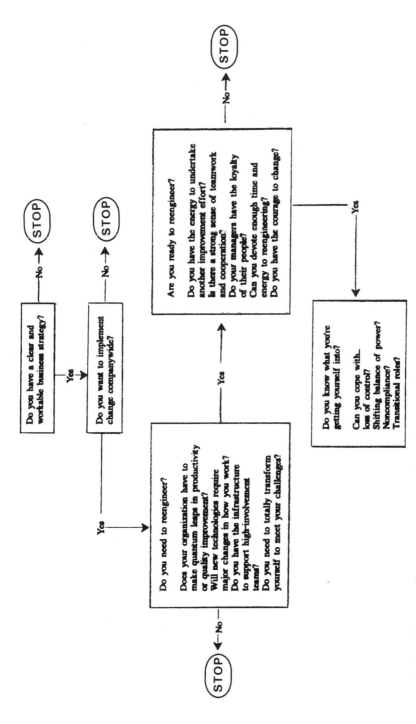

FIGURE 2.7. The Reengineering Decision Matrix

Do you have a clear and workable business strategy?

No → STOP

Yes

Do you want to implement change companywide?

No → STOP

Yes

Do you need to reengineer?

Does your organization have to make quantum leaps in productivity or quality improvement?
Will new technologies require major changes in how you work?
Do you have the infrastructure to support high-involvement teams?
Do you need to totally transform yourself to meet your challenges?

No → STOP

Yes

Are you ready to reengineer?

Do you have the energy to undertake another improvement effort?
Is there a strong sense of teamwork and cooperation?
Do your managers have the loyalty of their people?
Can you devote enough time and energy to reengineering?
Do you have the courage to change?

No → STOP

Yes

Do you know what you're getting yourself into?

Can you cope with—
loss of control?
Shifting balance of power?
Noncompliance?
Transitional roles?

Notes

1.   See Robert Frigo and Robert Janson, "GE's Financial Services Operation Achieves Quality Results Through 'Work-Out' Process," *National Productivity Review* (Winter 1993/94): pp. 53–61.

3

Where to Start: Preparing Your Organization to Reengineer

After they make the decision to reengineer, many top executives proceed to manage their change effort in much the same way as any other organizational project: They appoint a task force, delegate the responsibilities of implementation, and then wait patiently for the group to report back with recommendations and results. In most cases, this approach virtually guarantees that the change effort will fail. For no matter how committed or enthusiastic people are at the start, a reengineering effort will go nowhere unless the change process is truly championed all the way through.

We have known executives with exceptional administrative and operational skills who were poor at managing transformation efforts. How is that possible? Because leading change is not like any other managerial task. For one thing, it often requires that executives adopt a new role within their organization—that of "change agent"—and that they learn to practice a completely different set of skills and abilities.

One of the most critical is being able to deal well with people's emotions. Like anything else that requires major change, reengineering is bound to evoke plenty of fears and insecurities. At every level, people will ask: Is reengineering really necessary? What will it do for me? What will it do *to* me?

Any top executive who wants to reengineer must confront these worries head on and work vigorously to turn them around. And we believe that there's really only one way that can be done: by educating people thoroughly about what reengineering is, why you need to do it, and how it's going to be carried out (Figure 3.1).

---

1. What is reengineering?

2. Why do we need to do it?

3. What probable impact will it have?

4. How is it going to be carried out?

FIGURE 3.1. Educating Your Organization: Questions to Discuss

That does not necessarily mean that everyone in the organization has to attend 4-day reengineering workshops. But it does require a strong commitment to communicate openly and regularly. You have to be willing to explain—frequently and in language that everyone can understand—what the organization is being asked to take on, the possible impact it may have on people, and why it's necessary.

Never underestimate the degree of anxiety that the announcement of a major change effort will trigger. Even when you feel good about the decision to change—and look forward to tackling the hard work involved in finding a more efficient and more effective way to do business—remember that most of the people around you will be sitting nervously on the edge of their seats, expecting the worst that can possibly happen.

Because reengineering often has been linked with severe cost cutting and downsizing, the mere prospect of doing it can make people nervous. And they become especially apprehensive when it follows too quickly on the heels of a failed change effort or one that involved substantial streamlining. Just how anxious can people become? One example comes from a bank that wanted to reengineer to position itself for a merger or acquisition and had initiated an organizationwide effort to reduce overall costs by 20 percent in 18 months. Although the change effort was designed as a participative process, anxieties ran so high that one employee was driven to anonymously draft and release a bogus corporate policy memo that encouraged people to save money when traveling on company business by imposing on friends or relatives for lodging or by sleeping under a cozy overpass.

Conducting High-Level Discussions

The best way to begin the reengineering process is to conduct a series of preliminary discussions at the highest management levels to explain reengineering, justify its use, and promote its benefits (Figure 3.2). The rationale behind this strategy is obvious: No executive can hope to manage a change effort as complex as reengineering without the help of other leaders in the organization. Securing their commitment is essential for two reasons: (1) They are the ones who make the decisions allocating the time, resources, and people that make change happen, and (2) without their support, it's unlikely that those they manage will work to make change succeed.

Who should be included in these discussions often depends on the scope of the changes being considered. In any broad transformational effort, where multiple functions will be involved, the highest management body in the organization—the steering committee, or whatever the senior executive team is called—should participate. However, if reengineering will have an impact on only one or two departments—underwriting and claims, for example, but not sales, policy services, or any important support functions—then only those executives who head up the affected areas may have to be included.

- Explain what reengineering is.

- Justify its use.

- Promote its benefits.

- Build commitment to change.

- Overcome executive resistance.

- Achieve consensus on strategic change issues.

FIGURE 3.2.   Before Reengineering: Goals of Upper
Management Discussions

43

It's important to remember that reengineering often produces ripple effects: Changes introduced in one area, especially a line function that's critical to the business, can have repercussions in other departments, in support functions (usually information services and human resources), or throughout the entire organization. So it makes sense to include in these discussions executives whose jurisdiction may fall outside the defined scope of the project but whose work might be affected in some way by the change effort, or whose input or support might prove valuable later on.

Overcoming Executive Resistance

In time, these high-level meetings will be used to achieve consensus on the strategic issues relating to change: how long it will take, how participative it should be, or what departments and functions will be involved. But first they will provide the platform the chief executive needs to really sell the idea of reengineering and build commitment to the change effort.

Some resistance should be anticipated even at this level. Why? The reason is because in many organizations executives are just as unreceptive to change as anyone else and for the same reasons: They are afraid of losing their job or having to take on new responsibilities. And when the change strategy being considered is reengineering, there's a strong possibility that either of these may happen. One company, for example, decided to eliminate its functional structure when it reengineered and to reorganize along product lines. When the process was over, 25 of its top 26 managers had different job titles and new reporting relationships.

Winning over reluctant executives to the idea of reengineering may require one-on-one meetings or behind-the-scenes discussions. But, in general, the best way to persuade managers to endorse a reengineering effort is to educate them fully in two critical areas: (1) the value reengineering can bring to the organization and (2) how the reengineering process will be carried out.

Selling the Benefits of Reengineering

Executives are much less likely to oppose reengineering once they realize what it can mean to their organization in terms of better service, higher quality, and increased profits. Already there are a wealth of companies that can be used as examples to show just how reengineering can help to overcome systemic problems and increase competitive advantage (see Chapter 1, Figure 1.4).

We like to represent the benefits of reengineering through what we call the "C.E.O." diagram (Figure 3.3). It shows graphically how reengineering works and why it succeeds—that is, by having a significant and positive impact on all three major constituents of change: the customer (through improved service and higher quality), the employee (through more challenging and more satisfying jobs), and the organization (through increased productivity and profitability). In fact, we often encourage redesign teams to practice "C.E.O. thinking" throughout the reengineering process by asking themselves three critical questions whenever they propose a change or solution: How do the customers benefit? How do the employees benefit? How does the organization benefit?

- *How do the customers benefit?*

- *How do the employees benefit?*

- *How does the organization benefit?*

FIGURE 3.3. C.E.O. Diagram

Outlining Reengineering Principles and Activities

Another way to make executives more comfortable with the idea of reengineering is to help them understand exactly what's involved in bringing about organizational change. Once they see that there's a definite structure to the process—that it follows certain principles, that it can be broken down into specific activities, and that it can, in fact, be *managed*—many of their worst fears dissipate.

Outlining the basic principles of reengineering (Figure 3.4) can be reassuring because it convinces executives that the process addresses today's most pressing business imperatives (for example, by being customer-focused, by achieving strategic goals, and by promoting empowerment and responsibility). But it also provides a solid foundation for change that helps executives feel more secure: They know that as they proceed to reengineer, at least they will have a checklist they can use to gauge whether or not they're on the right track.

Outlining the eight major steps involved in a large-scale change effort (Figure 3.5) can also bring a deeper level of understanding. Although many of these steps are not unique to reengineering, they provide a mental construct executives can use to better grasp the process of change, and they describe in

---

1. Make the customer the starting point for change.

2. Design work processes in light of organizational goals.

3. Reorganize to support front-line performance.

4. Empower employees to make decisions in favor of the customer.

5. Partner with the customer in a long-term relationship.

FIGURE 3.4. Reengineering Principles

1. **Orchestrate dissatisfaction—**
   begin a process of critical self-examination.

2. **Keep it line driven—**
   encourage line managers to play an active role.

3. **Bring everyone into the room—**
   invite people at all levels to participate.

4. **Assess the present—**
   conduct a formal diagnosis of where you are and how you need to change.

5. **Design your future state—**
   envision what the company will look like at the end of the change process.

6. **Build a "gap" plan—**
   develop a clear implementation strategy.

7. **Implement—**
   carry out reforms and changes.

8. **Monitor and evaluate—**
   ensure that progress is being made and success targets are being achieved.

FIGURE 3.5.   Eight Steps to Companywide Change

general the type of activities that are involved in transforming any organization from what it has been into what it wants to become.

The Five Phases of Reengineering

There's yet another framework that can be used to educate and enlighten executives, and it's the one we rely on most. It defines organizational change as a process in five sequential phases (Figure 3.6): (1) plan and position, (2) diagnose, (3) redesign, (4) implement change, and (5) evaluate results.

Again, these phases can apply to any major change strategy. But the specific steps each phase comprises will vary significantly depending on the change strategy being implemented. In planning and positioning to reengineer, for example, there are four key *steps* involved:

- establish the scope and parameters
- determine success targets and measures
- identify project resources
- develop an initial plan

In this chapter, we will describe these steps and explain what needs to be done to execute them successfully.

Establish Reengineering Scope and Parameters

A primary responsibility of the executive team at the start of a reengineering effort is to establish boundaries for the change process (Figure 3.7). Early on, decisions must be made on what areas of the organization need to change, how much time can be devoted to reengineering, and how much of the organization will participate.

To some purists, this exercise may seem to contradict the true spirit of reengineering. After all, they might argue, the whole point of reengineering is to implement change *without* regard to existing limitations—to "blank slate" the future of your organization, to start from scratch, and to totally reinvent it the way you want it to be. Only then can you hope to achieve the dramatic breakthroughs in productivity, quality, and customer service that reengineering is famous for.

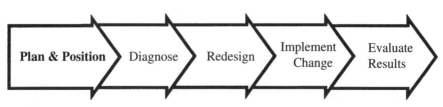

FIGURE 3.6.   The Five Phases of Reengineering

- What do we want to accomplish?

- How much time do we have to reengineer?

- What areas of the organization do we want to change?

FIGURE 3.7.   Step 1: Define Scope and Parameters

We agree that the goal of reengineering is to introduce radical change. But experience has shown that the realities of corporate life are such that, no matter what change strategy is chosen, there will always be some restrictions on what can be accomplished. If an organization has made a strategic technology decision, invested $6 million in a new computer system, and is halfway through the conversion process, it is not likely that it will scrap the entire project just because it has decided to reengineer.

There may also be logistical limitations that narrow your range of change options. Moving to another part of the country could help you to save on labor costs or a new facility might make certain production processes more efficient. But neither may be possible in the near future because you are locked into long-term leasing arrangements.

Defining the Change Effort

In any organization, there are three important issues the executive team must discuss in order to finalize the scope and parameters of a reengineering effort.

Change objectives. Before any changes can be implemented, the executive team must first agree on what needs to change and what it wants to accomplish through reengineering. It is not necessary to establish precise targets yet, but there must be consensus on the overall direction for change and general agreement on where the company wants to go.

At this early stage, change objectives should always be defined in terms of customer needs and expectations. Do you want to improve service by reducing turnaround time on new policy issues, for example? Do you want to reduce complaints by improving your speed and accuracy in filling orders? Do you want to increase market share by developing more innovative products and by manufacturing them more quickly? Remember, if your customers see no real benefit from the changes you make, then what you are doing is not reengineering.

Change timetable. Deciding how long the reengineering process should take usually depends on how fast a company wants to change and how soon it needs to see results, though experience over the past few years indicates that in this area of reengineering, the bar has been raised considerably. What used to be a 3- to 5-year process is now down to 12 to 18 months, and an organization that's in serious trouble—and must reengineer in order to survive—may pull out all the stops and implement improvements even more quickly.

In general, the entire process—from diagnosis to redesign to implementation—can be completed in 18 months, and when only a single business process is involved, it requires no more than 6 months. Given the complexity of reengineering, it's unlikely that you will see major gains in less than half a year. But you should not plan to drag the process out for too long, either. If you do, the market conditions you were responding to at the start may be significantly different when you finish, rendering many of your changes obsolete.

Change boundaries. The executive team must also decide which parts of the organization should be included in the reengineering effort—that is, what changes are going to be made and what units, departments, or divisions need to be involved in order to bring them about. Will it be necessary to include product development and customer service, for example, as well as sales and marketing? What will be the probable impact on operations, and does it suggest that they, too, should be involved from the start?

Reengineering is a creative process, of course, so it's not possible to predict at the outset exactly how work processes will change or what their ramifications will be. But you should at least establish some broad parameters of change just so you know who should participate in the change effort and who should be involved in making change-related decisions.

Determine Reengineering Success Targets

The second step in the planning and positioning phase is to establish specific targets for the reengineering effort (Figure 3.8). Once again, this is a direction-setting exercise that should be completed by the executive team or by the group of senior managers who will be most affected by reengineering.

This is a critical step in the change process, because what you finally achieve through reengineering is often a strong reflection of what you set out to do. Many companies end up with weak results because they establish too

- Focus on the three constituents of change.

- Quantify the results you are looking for.

- Establish "stretch" targets.

FIGURE 3.8. Step 2: Determine Success Targets

few success targets at the start, because they fail to quantify their targets, or because the targets they choose are too easily attained.

To help companies avoid these pitfalls, we recommend these guidelines for establishing reengineering targets:

Focus on the three constituents of change. When companies are asked what they want to achieve through reengineering, many answer with a single goal: We want to cut costs, they will say, or improve the quality of our customer service. But those that are really serious about reengineering respond with more complicated answers. They know that the only way to bring about truly *systemic* results—to achieve significant and lasting change—is to seek improvements all throughout their organization.

One way to make that happen is by practicing the "C.E.O. thinking" when setting reengineering goals. That way, the executive team will be sure to focus on all three constituents of change and establish improvement targets that are meaningful and broad-based. The three questions the team should ask are: What impact do we want to have on our customers? What impact do we want to have on our employees? What impact do we want to have on our organization?

Quantify the results you are looking for. To establish a clear agenda for reengineering, it's important to set quantitative targets for each of your change constituents. Ask yourself, for example: By how much do we want to improve turnaround time in filling customer orders? By how much do we want to reduce employee turnover? By how much do we want to improve the organization's productivity?

Deciding what these numbers should be is not always easy, because the executive team often has to work from poor or nonexistent baseline measurements. Although most companies collect extensive amounts of data to gauge their efficiency and profitability, assessments of customer satisfaction are usually more haphazard and less precise. And reliable indicators of employee motivation, job satisfaction, and readiness for change are rarer still.

Not knowing how customers view your organization or what they expect from your product or service makes it difficult to determine where you need to improve. And without accurate employee information, it's impossible to know which changes should be made to increase job satisfaction. For these reasons, it's sometimes necessary to conduct new surveys, interviews, or focus groups with customers and employees before reengineering targets can be finalized.

Establish "stretch" targets. The more incremental a company's approach to reengineering, the narrower the thinking that propels its change process and the less likely it will achieve significant results. If people are to demonstrate the type of creative thinking that will bring real organizational breakthroughs, ambitious goals have to be set for them.

What kind of numbers are we talking about? In applying traditional problem-solving or continuous improvement techniques, you can expect to achieve gains in efficiency and effectiveness of anywhere between 5 and 25 percent, depending on your starting point. But it's not uncommon for organizations that reengineer to set improvement targets of at least 30 percent (to reduce cycle time, say, or cut administrative costs) and sometimes as high as 50 or 60 percent!

What makes these numbers attainable, of course, is that reengineering is a cross-functional improvement process. You can't count on a major turnaround in processing time or service quality when you overhaul a single unit or department. But the broader the scope of your change effort, the greater your potential for significant improvement and the more aggressive you can be when setting your targets.

Identify Reengineering Project Resources

After establishing the framework and objectives for change, the next important step in the reengineering effort is to select the people who will lead and direct it. In most organizations, this means appointing a senior-level steering team to oversee the entire process and recruiting a reengineering coordinator, usually someone from the middle-management ranks, who will manage the process from day to day (Figure 3.9).

- Reengineering Steering Team
  - refine success targets
  - develop project plan
  - identify resources
  - review change proposals
  - monitor progress
  - recognize achievements

- Reengineering Coordinator
  - manage logistical issues
  - advise senior management
  - liaison with outsiders
  - lead communications team
  - contact all departments

FIGURE 3.9. Step 3: Identify Project Resources

Reengineering steering team. When reengineering is implemented on a companywide basis, it's only natural that the executive team or steering committee for the organization act as the steering team for the effort. If only selected parts of the organization are to be reengineered, however, then the members of the reengineering steering team usually include only those key executives who will be affected by change.

The reengineering steering team is the primary driver of the change effort and, as such, has major responsibilities. Initially, it must refine the targets for expense reduction and quality improvement, develop a project plan, and identify the human and financial resources that will be needed to reengineer. Its ongoing duties are just as substantial: It must reinforce and stimulate project activities, review and approve change proposals, monitor progress, and continually recognize achievements. Without the constant vigilance and support of the steering team, the change effort is likely to flag and lose steam or, just as bad, veer in a direction that produces negligible or undesirable results.

Even though the steering team does not become involved in the tactical implementation of change, it's not uncommon for members to devote at least 30 percent of their time to performing reengineering-related activities—providing guidance and advice to redesign teams, following up on changes and reviewing results, removing organizational obstacles that hinder change, and making sure that reengineering is at the top of everyone's work agenda. By maintaining an active and highly visible role in the change process, the steering team reinforces the notion that reengineering has full management support and is a top organizational priority.

Where steering teams typically underperform are in planning and scheduling events to celebrate successes. Most companies don't do enough morale building, and that can be detrimental to their reengineering efforts. Remember that change can be a long and difficult process, and it's important to have fun every once in a while and take the time to feel good about what you have accomplished so far.

Reengineering coordinator. If the steering team can be said to provide the brains and backbone for the change effort, the reengineering coordinator provides the hands and feet. This person deals with many of the logistical issues involved with organizational change (making sure that meeting space is available, locating technical experts for teams, etc.), manages the communications program, and acts as a central contact for all the parties concerned. If outside consultants are used to facilitate the change process, the reengineering coordinator also serves as the company liaison with that group.

As the most visible player in the process, the reengineering coordinator is often seen as the person who embodies the spirit and values of the change effort (Figure 3.10). So it's important to pick someone who is well known in the organization and who is recognized as being hard-working, credible, capable, and fair. Some other characteristics you should look for include the following:

- strong organizational, interpersonal, and project-management skills

- an openness to new ideas and the ability to deal well with conflicting opinions

- a genuine desire to see the organization change and improve

Many companies choose a "rising star" from within their middle-management ranks—someone who's enthusiastic, energetic, and eager to gain exposure—to act as reengineering coordinator. This type of person usually has the vitality the position demands, but has not yet developed the entrenched attitudes that may signal a "hidden agenda." The job should never go to someone who's recently lost responsibilities and needs more work to do: This characterizes the position as a "time-filler" and dilutes the importance of the reengineering effort.

- Is recognized as hard-working, credible, and fair

- Is enthusiastic and energetic

- Has strong organizational, interpersonal, and project-management skills

- Is open to new ideas

- Deals well with conflicting opinions

- Wants to see the organization change and improve

FIGURE 3.10. Profile of Reengineering Coordinator

One of the best coordinators we ever worked with was an executive who was only 2 years away from retirement when his company began to reengineer. His age and company standing made him an unlikely candidate for the position, but he had a unique personality and demonstrated the kind of qualities that made him perfect for the job: He still wanted to learn and grow; he was highly curious about reengineering and the process of change; and he had a strong desire to leave his organization a legacy with which he could be proud.

Reengineering coordinators usually report directly to the steering team or, if the change effort is broad enough, to the president or CEO. They typically wear two hats—continuing to carry out at least some of the functional responsibilities they previously performed—and devote anywhere from 40 to 70 percent of their time to change-related activities.

In some companies (particularly when reengineering is limited to only a few departments), it's not uncommon for the coordinator to be involved in every aspect of diagnosis, redesign, and implementation, and for the position to be designated as full-time. In these cases, it's especially important to emphasize the transitional nature of the job. You do not want to create the impression of a reengineering "bureaucracy" or lead people to believe that reengineering is a process without end. Everyone should realize that the extra work they put in, the disruptions they endure, and the sacrifices they make for improvement all contribute to achieving specific results from which they—as well as the organization and its customers—will benefit.

Develop an Initial Reengineering Plan

The last step in the planning and positioning phase is the development of an initial reengineering plan (Figure 3.11). Two activities are required when you're planning to reengineer:

1. establish a preliminary timetable for the change process

2. develop a comprehensive internal public relations and communications strategy

A timetable is necessary to discipline the organization to complete the change process within a specified period of time. It allocates a certain number of weeks or months for each major phase of reengineering (3 months for diagnosis, say, 2 months for redesign, and 8 months for implementation), and it establishes provisional deadlines for the activities involved in each phase. Naturally, this timetable isn't written in stone—you may have to modify it as you go along—but at least it provides a general schedule you can follow and some target dates to shoot for.

Select the Best and the Brightest

Some people feel that setting deadlines at the very start of a reengineering effort is unrealistic or, even worse, counterproductive. They believe that change should be allowed to evolve naturally, that reengineering is a creative process that can't be forced, and that people need time to learn how to interact comfortably on teams. Some experts even claim that it may take some team mem-

---

- Establish a timetable for change.

- Develop a communications strategy.

FIGURE 3.11. Step 4: Develop an Initial Plan

bers up to 2 years before they adjust to their new roles completely and can begin to work with each other effectively.

We disagree. The primary purpose of reengineering is not just to bring about change, but to do it as quickly as possible. Many organizations that reengineer must see significant results within a year if they are to regain a competitive edge in their marketplace or maintain a leadership position. So establishing a timetable and target dates is for them not just an effective way to expedite change, it's an essential component of the reengineering planning process.

Nor does reengineering require special skills and abilities that people need a lot of time to learn and master. Most companies have been using task forces, committees, and other ad hoc work groups to solve problems for years, so many of their people already possess the skills they need to participate effectively on reengineering teams. What's more, those that do need help can turn to any number of resources during the reengineering process for expertise and support: the steering team, the reengineering coordinator, their team leader or facilitator, or outside consultants the company may have brought in.

People often learn new skills when their company reengineers, but that does not mean that the process should be viewed essentially as an opportunity for continued training and development. If it were, we would advise executives to recruit their most inexperienced people for membership on reengineering teams. Instead, we recommend just the opposite. Companies that reengineer should select their best and brightest people to participate, and choosing the right mix of people—those who have extensive knowledge, exceptional skills, and positive attitudes—is the only way to ensure significant and timely results through reengineering.

Make Communications a Priority

Developing a comprehensive communications strategy during the planning and positioning phase is also critical to the success of reengineering. Most organizations minimize the importance of communications when they begin to reengineer, and all too many of them later regret it. Although CEOs and presidents are often told that they can never communicate too much, they inevitably look back 6 months into the reengineering process and wish they had done more.

Regular and frequent communication is essential all throughout reengineering, but it's especially important at the start, when you are trying to establish the rationale for change and build buy-in to the change process. Most executives underestimate what it takes to do this. They think that if they simply explain the company's reasons for reengineering in an eloquent speech or memo, they will succeed at getting their point across and people will rally to the reengineering cause. But research shows that employees rarely grasp the importance of management announcements the first time around, and that they often have to hear the same message over and over again before it sinks in.

Companies also rely far too much on vision statements to kick off their reengineering efforts. Executives sometimes spend weeks preparing inspirational documents that were intended to explain—as concisely and poetically as possible—what their company's goals are for reengineering and what values the company will follow during the change process. Yet no matter how carefully crafted or prominently displayed, these expressions of corporate "poetry" usually have little or no impact.

Issuing a fancy and official-looking document is certainly not the best way to win support for implementing a major change strategy. A far more effective approach is to sit down with small groups of people, explain what the company is thinking of doing, and give them a chance to respond to what you say.

That's what managers did at General Electric's Financial Services Operation (FSO).[1] When they decided to reengineer in the late 1980s, they conducted a series of informal "town meetings"—open to all employees—at every FSO location in the country. These lively question-and-answer sessions accomplished two important goals: They raised awareness of why the organization had to change, and they showed people how they had to work differently in order to bring about change.

Managers who conduct meetings like these should ask two key questions: (1) What gets you excited about what we're thinking of doing? (2) What are your concerns? Giving people the opportunity to voice their thoughts and reactions sends the message that you are interested in what they have to say and willing to listen to their ideas. But it also provides you with valuable information: about what kinds of resistance you can anticipate, who the natural leaders are in your organization, and how prepared your people are to reengineer.

Take the Organizational Pulse

The most successful companies use a two-way communications strategy all throughout their reengineering effort. They make the commitment not only to keep people informed of what's going on but also to find out what people are feeling and thinking about it.

One way these companies carry out this pledge is by establishing an internal communications team that acts as a conduit for information from above and from below. Usually led or recruited by the reengineering coordinator, this team is often composed of members from several different levels in the organization who dedicate a small amount of their time (5 to 10 percent) to communications activities related specifically to reengineering.

To help them decide what they want to do, communications teams typically conduct preliminary sessions where they brainstorm answers to questions like: Who are the audiences to which we will be communicating? What communication vehicles have worked well for us in the past? How often will we need to issue updates? These discussions often lead to major team decisions—to publish a reengineering newsletter, for example, to hold a kickoff event to launch the reengineering effort, or to schedule periodic town meetings.

Newsletters are especially good for communicating messages from management and for squelching rumors, and meetings provide an effective platform for addressing employees' confusions and frustrations. Whatever forms of communication the team uses, however, it's important for employees to know that they can voice their concerns and get answers to questions, and for executives to feel confident that there's a system in place for monitoring the organizational pulse.

Notes

1.   See Robert Frigo and Robert Janson, "GE's Financial Services Operation Achieves Quality Results Through 'Work-Out' Process," *National Productivity Review* (Winter 1993/94): pp. 53–61.

4

Groundwork for Redesign: Conducting an Organizational Diagnosis

One of the most hotly debated issues in reengineering these days is whether companies should conduct an initial diagnosis before they reengineer, or whether they should ignore their existing structures and work processes altogether and redesign from scratch. A number of strong and convincing arguments have been made by the so-called "blank-slate" group of thinkers. Chief among their claims is that diagnosis is an impediment to radical change because it encourages people to focus on what already exists rather than what might possibly be.

We agree that unrestricted creativity and innovation are critical when your objective is to become something different from what you've been before. And by its very nature, reengineering seems to favor the antidiagnosis school. But we also see important benefits to diagnosis, and in just about every case, we recommend it. Why? Our position isn't based on philosophical grounds. We have simply learned from experience that when companies undertake change, those that diagnose themselves beforehand seem to do a better job of reengineering than those that do not (Figure 4.1). In hindsight, there are several reasons why this might be true (Figure 4.2).

Diagnosis establishes a starting point for change. In order to reengineer successfully, you have to develop a vision of what you want to become when the change process is over. But there's no way you can determine how to get there unless you know exactly where you are starting from and understand the

61

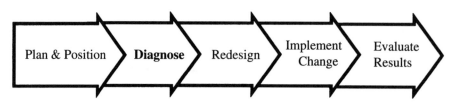

FIGURE 4.1. The Five Phases of Reengineering

"gap" between the future you hope to bring about and the reality you live in now. Diagnosis helps identify where your reengineering journey begins and gives a good idea of the amount of work involved in getting where you want to go.

Diagnosis promotes a customer-centered perspective. Most organizations gauge their effectiveness on internal measures: number of phone calls answered per hour, for example, or case load per worker. Others use external criteria to evaluate their performance: How well does the organization operate, in other words, from the customer's point of view? A good diagnosis incorporates both perspectives. It allows people to see—often for the very first time—just how good their organization is at translating the work it performs into feelings of customer satisfaction.

Diagnosis provides a cross-functional education. No matter how bright or creative the people are who have been chosen to lead and implement change, few will possess the cross-functional perspective that reengineering requires. Even if recruits are limited to those who serve regularly on task forces and committees, chances are that most of them will be functional specialists with only a partial understanding of how your company operates.

One advantage to conducting a diagnosis is that it provides an educational opportunity for people. In trying to understand what works well in the organization and what needs to change, many of them will be exposed to departments or units they didn't know much about before, and they will develop a broader knowledge of their business as a whole.

Diagnosis stimulates feelings of "positive dissatisfaction." Making the decision to reengineer doesn't guarantee the support of everyone you will need to make your change effort succeed. There will always be those who say they feel comfortable with the way things are now and see no reason to reengineer. Although their resistance may be founded more on fear than logic, it's un-

- To establish a starting point for change.

- To develop a customer-centered perspective.

- To provide a cross-functional education.

- To stimulate feelings of positive dissatisfaction.

- To identify potential quick hits.

- To promote involvement in the change process.

FIGURE 4.2. Reasons for Diagnosing

likely they will make a commitment to change unless they are convinced that the organization is faltering, that you are falling behind your competition, or that major improvements in product and service quality are necessary.

A formal diagnosis helps you orchestrate feelings of "positive dissatisfaction" with the current organization, and that increases the overall motivation to change. By bringing existing problems to light and by uncovering opportunities for improvement, diagnosis stimulates the desire for change and mobilizes the kind of energy you need to reengineer.

Diagnosis identifies potential quick hits. Reengineering may be a long and demanding process, but not all the changes you make when you reengineer involve a lot of work. Companies sometimes realize that they can save considerable time and resources simply by eliminating a report that no one reads, for example, or by reordering the steps in a critical process. Diagnosis often helps identify these potential "quick hits." And by allowing them to happen at the start of the change process, it accelerates the pace of reengineering, helps people to feel they are making headway early on, and provides a welcome boost to organizational morale.

Diagnosis encourages involvement in the change process. Companies that reengineer should seek to actively involve as many employees as possible in both the planning and implementation stages of their transformation effort.

Not only does this build buy-in to change, it also establishes a larger pool of creative thinkers you can draw from for new ideas and suggestions.

Diagnosis helps promote participation by asking employees from all levels to analyze strengths and weaknesses, uncover potential problems, and identify opportunities for improvement. Though not everyone is included when conducting an organizational diagnosis, carrying out the process helps widen the circle of involvement and encourages more people to feel that they share the responsibility for change.

The Diagnostic Snapshot: How Big a Picture?

One of the most frequent questions companies ask when they reengineer is how much should they cover when they conduct a diagnosis? Their concerns are understandable. A diagnosis that attempts too much can waste valuable time and resources, lead a reengineering effort down unproductive paths, or divert the organization from its day-to-day obligations. But a diagnosis that's too narrow can also present dangers: It may overlook significant opportunities for improvement or exclude parts of the organization that may later prove critical to change (Figure 4.3).

When the diagnostic snapshot is too wide	When the diagnostic snapshot is too narrow
• The diagnosis wastes time and resources. • The diagnosis leads you down unproductive paths. • The diagnosis diverts you from day-to-day obligations.	• The diagnosis overlooks opportunities for improvements. • The diagnosis excludes areas that may later prove critical to change.

FIGURE 4.3. Problems with Diagnostic Snapshots

This issue may not arise in companies where an entire division or business unit (the commercial loan section of a bank, for example, or an insurance carrier's life business) is to undergo change; there the parameters for diagnosis are easily defined. But when a company doesn't yet know exactly what it wants to reengineer and has trouble defining the boundaries of change, this is the advice we usually offer: Diagnose as much as you can, but do it as quickly and as efficiently as possible.

In principle, we feel it's better to have more knowledge than less, and a broader diagnosis simply allows you to make better reengineering decisions. Though you may not always be able to act on the information you uncover (because of limited resources, perhaps), at least you will know that the priorities you establish will be based on a comprehensive assessment.

There's also no way of knowing at the start just what your diagnosis will reveal. Many companies come to the conclusion at the end of their diagnosis that there's more for them to reengineer than they originally believed. Several insurance companies, for example, chose to leave out their sales and distribution staffs when they drew up their preliminary reengineering plans. But these functions were incorporated into the scope of their change projects after a diagnosis was conducted. The reason: The diagnosis pointed out that parts of their organizations that seemed to be working fine exhibited serious flaws when they were looked at from the customer's point of view.

There's one major pitfall that must be avoided when conducting a comprehensive diagnosis, however, and that's the tendency to become bogged down in the analytical process. It's all too easy for organizations—especially those made up of strong analytical thinkers, like banks and insurance companies—to linger in the diagnostic phase of reengineering and delay the more creative, and usually more demanding, phase of organizational redesign.

How can you keep from slipping into "analysis paralysis"? The best way is to develop a strong diagnostic plan, one that clearly outlines the responsibilities of the diagnostic team, the time frame it has to work in, its targets for diagnosis, and the tools it will use to get the job done (Figure 4.4).

The Diagnostic Team

The diagnostic team, selected by the steering team, should represent all those areas within the organization that are to be reengineered. The size of the team will depend on the scope of the change effort: Diagnostic teams can comprise as few as 6 members or as many as 30.

- Outlines the responsibilities of the diagnostic team

- Establishes a time frame for diagnosis

- Identifies the diagnostic targets

- Identifies the diagnostic tools

FIGURE 4.4. The Diagnostic Plan

The diagnostic team performs a critical and highly visible role at the start of the reengineering process, so it's important to select team members who will succeed at the job and lend credibility to the change effort (Figure 4.5). They should be well organized and have strong analytical, interviewing, and data-gathering skills. They should have an in-depth knowledge of their own area, but also possess some understanding of the business as a whole. Finally, they should be able to function well on a team.

Every major constituency in the departments or units to be reengineered should be represented on the diagnostic team. But it also helps to include some technical professionals—especially if major systems changes are anticipated—as well as managers from the sales, service, or marketing areas. Because of their front-line experience, these people usually possess a stronger customer focus than others, and they add a valuable perspective to the diagnostic work. Managers who are highly specialized, however, or who supervise only a narrow portion of the work to be diagnosed are not good candidates for team membership.

The Diagnostic Mandate

The first order of business in conducting a diagnosis is to assemble the members of the diagnostic team and make sure they clearly understand what their charge is. When teams perform weak or inadequate diagnoses, it's usually because they see the process simply as an investigative or data-gathering exercise. They fail to realize that the primary purpose of their work is to trans-

- Represents a constituency of change

- Has strong analytical, interviewing, and data-gathering skills

- Is well-organized

- Demonstrates a broad knowledge of the business

- Clearly understands the team's charge

- Can adhere to a firm timetable

- Works well on a team

FIGURE 4.5. Profile of a Diagnostic Team Member

form the data they collect into the kind of information the organization can use to drive the reengineering effort.

The work of the diagnostic team should be guided by three major questions:

1. What does our organization do well?
2. What is it that we don't do well?
3. What are the opportunities for improvement?

And the team should attempt to answer each of these questions from the points of view of the three reengineering stakeholders: the customer, the employee, and the organization. Only by applying a multiple perspective can the team achieve the comprehensive analysis that a major change effort requires.

The Diagnostic Timetable

Another major responsibility of the diagnostic team is to adhere to a firm timetable for completion, one that's usually determined by the steering team at the start of the diagnostic phase. How long does diagnosis typically last? We recommend that diagnostic teams be required to submit their final report (or make a presentation) no later than 12 weeks after they begin their work.

To some, this may seem like a harsh or unrealistic stipulation, especially in large organizations, where diagnosis can pose significant logistical challenges. But most teams are able to meet this deadline—and some with time to spare. Granted, diagnosis usually involves a great deal of hard work and running around, but it's the kind of work that's exciting and energizing. And when diagnostic teams are made to realize the full importance of what they are doing, they are usually more motivated to do a good job and to complete their assignment on time.

It also helps to be well organized and to operate efficiently. Organizations are less likely to get "stuck" early on in the reengineering process if they have clearly identified targets for diagnosis and know beforehand exactly what diagnostic tools they need to use.

The Diagnostic Targets

Once the diagnostic team is formed and understands its mandate, how does it proceed? The first step is to identify the team's diagnostic targets: all those areas that must be covered in order to produce a comprehensive organizational snapshot. We strongly recommend that companies frame their diagnosis around these seven key issues (Figure 4.6).

Mission and goals. One important purpose in conducting a diagnosis is to evaluate how well your organization communicates its mission and goals and to determine what is in the way when people do not understand them. Some key questions to address are: Do employees demonstrate a basic knowledge of your customers, their needs and expectations, and the company's strategy for meeting them? Do employees have clear job objectives and ways to measure their success in reaching them? Do employees fully understand their role in carrying out the organization's mission?

Organizational structure. The diagnosis should also analyze what effect the structure of the company, the design of jobs, and the flow of work have on organizational efficiency, customer satisfaction, and employee motivation. How many layers of management do you have, for example, and how many are really needed? Does the current structure foster strong relationships between employees and customers? Do existing jobs encourage initiative and creativity and promote feelings of accountability at all levels? Does each job have a nat-

---

MISSION AND GOALS
- Do employees understand customer needs?
- Do employees have clear job objectives?
- Do employees understand their role in carrying out your mission?

ORGANIZATIONAL STRUCTURE
- How many layers of management do you have and how many are needed?
- Does the structure foster strong customer relationships?
- Does each job have a natural beginning and end?

QUALITY, SERVICE, AND PRODUCTIVITY
- Are there systems to identify customer expectations?
- Are customer expectations being met?
- Are you able to meet customer needs efficiently?

TECHNOLOGY
- Which functions need to be automated?
- Do people have the technology they need?
- Does your use of technology empower employees?

CULTURE AND STYLE
- Is there a history of teamwork?
- Are managers committed to participation?
- Does your culture promote innovation?

CONTROL SYSTEMS
- Do compensation systems promote corporate goals?
- Do recognition-and-reward systems encourage the right behaviors?
- Do measurement systems provide the information you need?

STRENGTHS AND WEAKNESSES
- What weaknesses need immediate attention?
- Are you capitalizing on your strengths?

FIGURE 4.6. Diagnostic Targets

ural beginning and end, or are people required to perform "incomplete" or fragmented work procedures?

Quality, service, and productivity. Your success at satisfying customer needs—and your ability to do it cost-effectively—is another area that should be included within the scope of your diagnosis. The key questions here are: Do you have systems in place to identify who your customers are and what they expect from you? How do customers compare your quality and service levels to those of your competitors? Are all customer expectations of quality and service being adequately met, or are some customers more satisfied than others? Are you able to meet customer needs efficiently, or do you spend a lot of time and resources performing rework and attempting to regain lost customers?

Technology. You should examine how effectively the organization uses technology to satisfy customers, improve jobs, and achieve organizational goals. For example, which of the functions needed to service your customers have not yet been automated? Do people feel that they have the technology they need to get their jobs done? Does your use of technology help to empower employees and allow them to make critical decisions? Can the systems you use to improve performance within specific units be adapted for use in other departments or functions?

Culture and style. The diagnosis must also focus on the so-called "soft" issues related to organizational effectiveness, such as corporate culture and management style, in order to examine the values and beliefs that guide people's behaviors. Are employee suggestions for improvement actively solicited and implemented, for example? Does the organization have a solid history of collaboration and teamwork? Do managers demonstrate a commitment to involvement and participation? Does the culture promote innovation and risk taking, or do existing management styles actually discourage these practices?

Control systems. The management tools that are used to keep your company operating smoothly on a day-to-day basis represent another aspect of the organization that must be looked at. These include all the systems that have been put in place to recognize or reward behaviors, or to monitor progress in achieving quality, productivity, or financial goals. Three questions may help to guide analysis here: Do your compensation systems work to promote your corporate goals? Do your recognition-and-reward systems encourage the kinds of behaviors that will assure your success? Do your measurement systems provide the information you need to gauge how well you are doing and to make improvements?

Strengths and weaknesses. Finally, you should evaluate your organization's overall strengths and weaknesses in relation to your reengineering goals. Without such an analysis, you will find it more difficult to establish priorities for change and to determine where to invest your limited time and resources.

Naturally, it helps to know which areas of weakness need to be addressed immediately and which ones you can work on later. But your organization's strengths also must be analyzed for their strategic value. It's not impossible that money and manpower are being diverted into areas that may actually have little impact on organizational success.

The Diagnostic Tools

All too often, organizations that reengineer base their change recommendations on a single diagnostic tool: a work flow analysis, perhaps, or a customer questionnaire. But we don't believe you can conduct a comprehensive diagnosis using just one tool. To confirm trends across organizational boundaries and levels—and to compare what your customers are saying to what's happening *inside* your company—you have to generate a lot of information, and that usually requires multiple tools and techniques. There are six that provide a solid basis for making decisions about reengineering changes (Figure 4.7).

Existing data sources. Most organizations that reengineer have collected data within the previous 6 to 12 months that may prove valuable to the diagnostic team: a recent customer poll, for example, or an internal climate survey. New production and financial figures—such as defect rates, productivity statistics, and profit-and-loss numbers, as well as data on turnover, labor grievances, and the like—could also prove helpful, though much of it may be department-specific. The team should not review information that's more than a year old because it may no longer be relevant.

Existing data sources can save the diagnostic team considerable time and energy; after all, there's no need to duplicate data that already exists. But the team must make sure that the sources it includes are drawn from areas that fall within the scope of the change effort and that they clearly contribute to a better understanding of the reengineering issues being targeted.

Customer feedback. Though some companies perform periodic surveys of the people who buy their products or services, efforts to gather reliable and up-to-date information about customers on a regular basis are weak in most organizations, especially in those areas that badly need reengineering. So in many cases, a diagnostic team must develop new instruments to solicit input from customers and to evaluate their needs and expectations.

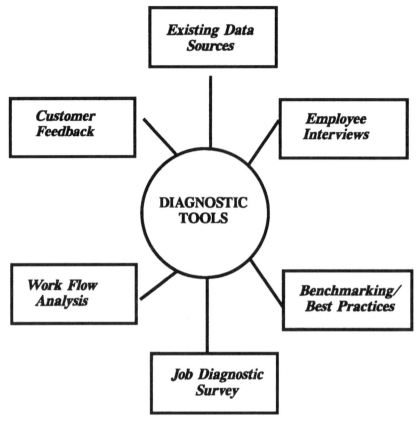

FIGURE 4.7. Diagnostic Tools

What customers should be contacted? Clearly, the time constraints of this reengineering phase do not allow the diagnostic team to mount a major customer-feedback study. But quick and inexpensive surveys conducted by mail or by phone—or structured focus-group sessions—can usually be completed within the time allotted. The secret to their success: Choose representative buyers from within each customer segment to talk to, or interview those customers who are responsible for most of your sales revenues.

Social or informal contacts with customers—industry conferences that happen to take place during the diagnostic phase, for example—may also provide valuable opportunities to tap into what your customers think. And if dealing directly with customers is just too difficult or costly, talk to the people within your organization who work with them most often and who know them best: your sales and marketing people, for example, or your front-line service providers.

Employee interviews. Formal surveys conducted internally are another powerful way to uncover vital information about what's working well in your organization and what isn't. To make the most of this tool, however, we recommend scheduling personal interviews or conducting small focus groups rather than distributing written questionnaires. Although they take more time (an average of 40 to 50 minutes each), face-to-face sessions provide more valuable information: Not only do they give respondents the chance to explain what they mean and to clarify their answers, they also allow interviewers to pick up nonverbal messages through voice tone, facial gestures, and body language.

Employee surveys should be highly structured and cover all the areas the team has identified as diagnostic targets. There could be a series of questions related to the organization's mission and goals, for example, as well as questions on organizational structure, technology, control systems, and so forth. We like to insert a few questions at the end of the session that permit people to bring up issues the survey may have overlooked or that help them to speak more freely. Examples: "Are there any topics we haven't covered that you'd like to discuss?" "If you could change anything about this organization, what would you change and why?"

It's not uncommon for diagnostic teams to survey up to 50 percent of all employees in this manner, though 20 percent is an adequate sample, as long as it represents all the functions, levels, and departments to be reengineered. Employees who are not selected as part of the sample but who express a strong desire to be interviewed should be included. It's also a good idea to send out a letter or memo before the interviews take place to inform employees that they have their manager's permission to participate, to encourage them to be honest in their responses, and to reassure them that their responses will remain confidential.

Work flow analysis. A high-level analysis of the tasks and activities that make up individual work processes is essential to a comprehensive diagnosis. Before reengineering changes and improvements can be made, it's important to understand what transactions and procedures make up a work process, why they are performed, and in what order (Figure 4.8).

Although information on work flows is often on file in many organizations, how work is actually carried out may differ significantly from work designs on paper. That's why it always helps to talk directly to the people who perform the work: Assemble representatives from the areas involved to talk through the

- What's the logic used in planning the work flow?

- Do "whole" jobs exist, or is the work fragmented?

- Does the division of labor establish accountabilities clearly?

- What are the sources of feedback on work performance?

- How often is work checked or verified, and do these functions contribute to work quality?

- Do people exercise judgment and control in their jobs, or is that the responsibility of supervisors?

- Are there redundant or unnecessary functions?

- How long does work sit in waiting stages between process steps?

FIGURE 4.8.   Work Flow Analysis: Key Diagnostic Questions

process under review, or literally walk through those parts of the organization that contribute work to the process and record what people are doing.

It's not necessary to document every move an employee makes or every subtask that's performed. A fully documented work flow analysis can be extremely complex, so try to focus on those characteristics that determine the *effectiveness* of the work flow: How many employees are required to complete the process? How many times does the customer need to be contacted? How long does the process take, and where are the delays and bottlenecks?

Many new software products are now being introduced that help organizations chart work flows. Some are easy to use, and others are extremely complex. We recommend that you opt for simplicity. The reason: Although a few people in your organization may be able to master the complicated programs, it will take a significant amount of time to train and coach others in how to use them, and that can delay the data-gathering process. Besides, we have found that much of what you need to know from conducting a work flow analysis can be learned from the intelligent use of paper and pencil.

Job diagnostic survey. Another tool to measure the effectiveness of work design is the Job Diagnostic Survey (JDS). Originally developed by a Yale professor and inspired by the work of behavioral scientist Frederick Herzberg, the JDS seeks to answer three key questions: What is the motivational value of the job? What are the achievement and personal growth needs of the person doing it? And how well are these needs satisfied in the job as it's currently designed?

The JDS is based on the theory that there are five core job dimensions that contribute to job satisfaction and motivation: skill variety, task identity, task significance, autonomy, and feedback (see Chapter 1). Using survey questions to measure these dimensions quantitatively, the JDS indicates which dimensions are most in need of improvement and generates a summary score for each job that reflects its overall "motivating potential" (Figure 4.9).

The JDS has been used for over 25 years, and it is still useful as a diagnostic tool. When used in conjunction with other analytical instruments, it provides crucial information for designing jobs that are both motivating and productive.

Several years ago at the First National Bank of Chicago, for example, the JDS showed that jobs in its commercial lending division frequently lacked autonomy and variety. And a recent application at New England Telephone Company revealed that employees in its Interexchange Customer Service Center had high professional growth needs and would respond well to new jobs. These results subsequently proved extremely valuable to reengineering teams in both organizations when they set out to redesign jobs and restructure work into new configurations.

---

1. Does your job permit you to decide on your own how to go about doing the work?

2. Does your job require you to use a variety of your skills and talents?

3. Does your job involve doing a complete piece of work, or is it only a small part of the overall process?

4. Do the results of your work significantly affect the lives or well-being of other people?

5. Does your work provide you with clues about how well you're doing, aside from any feedback from your manager?

FIGURE 4.9.   Sample Job Diagnostic Survey Questions

Benchmarking/best practices. Companies can also learn much about themselves by looking beyond their organizational boundaries—by examining what their competitors are doing, for example, or by studying exceptional performers in other industries. These tools, called "benchmarking" and "best practices," contribute an additional perspective to diagnosis that complements what you can discover from internal measurements, from employee interviews, and from customer surveys.

Benchmarking is a structured interview process that allows you to measure yourself against organizations within your own industry. Although a formal agreement usually has to be drawn up beforehand between the benchmarking "partners"—and restrictions are often placed on the release of proprietary information—more and more companies are taking advantage of this practice, even those in industries, like banking, that have been traditionally reluctant to share. Although extensive benchmarking studies can take several months or longer to complete, it is possible for a diagnostic team to benchmark with a select group of partners in just a couple of weeks.

Best practices is similar to benchmarking in that it encourages learning through external comparisons. But it focuses on specific functions or work processes and on the organizations that perform them best, whether or not they operate in your industry or provide a product or service similar to yours. An insurance company, for example, might learn a great deal from comparing its accounts payable practices to those in a computer company noted for its efficiency and timeliness in payment. Or a busy savings bank might benefit from studying how a top-ranked theme park handles long lines of waiting customers.

The Diagnostic Report

Some diagnostic teams organize their work by department or unit. One group of team members will apply all six tools to the marketing and sales department, for example, whereas another group will conduct a complete diagnosis of production and manufacturing. More often, however, teams will organize around the six diagnostic tools. There will be a work flow analysis subteam, an employee survey subteam, a benchmarking subteam, and so on. There are two advantages to this approach: When team members specialize in specific tools, the diagnosis is usually implemented with greater speed and proficiency, and each team member has a chance to conduct field work in every part of the organization.

No matter how the team is organized, completing all the tasks involved in a comprehensive diagnosis can be a major challenge, so it helps to draw up a week-by-week work plan to establish the interim deadlines that must be met *before* the presentation to the steering team (Figure 4.10). At the time they set out to gather information, all members of the diagnostic team should know exactly when they are going to reconvene to present and discuss their findings and when they should be prepared to conduct a cross-functional analysis, identify significant trends, and write the final report.

At this stage, careful planning and uncompromising deadlines are critical to the reengineering effort for two reasons. First, they provide the discipline that members of the diagnostic team need in order to complete the important job they're assigned to do. Second, they set a valuable precedent for the cross-functional teams that will be set up in the later phases of reengineering.

Analyzing the Diagnostic Findings

The key to a successful diagnosis is making sense of the vast amount of data that's collected, reporting back to the steering team on organizational trends and patterns, and then recommending specific reengineering changes. This is usually not too difficult to do, we have found, especially when diagnostic teams base their conclusions on the six tools described earlier. In most cases,

Key Task	Target Date
• Team training session	_____
• Subteam data gathering	_____
• Team checkpoint	_____
• Subteam analysis and presentation	_____
• Cross-functional analysis and trending	_____
• Writing up findings	_____
• Presentation to the steering team	_____

FIGURE 4.10.   Key Task Planner for Diagnostic Team

major problems with quality, service, or productivity will surface repeatedly, and the team will be able to identify them with ease.

In one company that reengineered, for example, managers had suspected that slow turnaround time was the primary reason for the company's mediocre service ratings. Sure enough, the diagnostic findings confirmed that improved responsiveness should be a major reengineering goal. Not only did customer feedback point to problems in this area, work flow analyses also indicated that cycle times were unnecessarily slow, and a quick benchmarking study showed that many of the company's competitors were considerably faster.

Presenting the Diagnostic Findings

The findings and recommendations of the diagnostic team are usually presented to the steering team at a formal management session, complete with slides or overheads and backup materials on each of the diagnostic tools used. A final report is also handed out to team members that presents, in a clear and well-organized way, the overall strengths and weaknesses of the organization, the major issues that it faces, and the most promising opportunities for change.

In many cases, the report of the diagnostic team is a real eye-opener for steering team members. Rarely do organizations examine themselves with such honesty and thoroughness, and when they do, the results can sometimes be startling. Often for the first time, executives are made aware of significant gaps between customer expectations and company performance, major disparities in service or quality levels among departments or units, and differences in morale and job satisfaction among organizational levels.

The diagnostic report provides an even greater stimulus for change once it's disseminated throughout the entire organization, and we firmly believe that its findings should not be restricted solely to senior management. Not only do others have a right to see the results of a process they participated in, everyone in the organization should be apprised of what was learned from the diagnosis and what it will mean for the change effort ahead. No matter what medium you use to communicate them—the company newsletter, perhaps, or small "town meetings"—the findings of the diagnostic team represent critical information to which everyone should have access.

First Diagnosis, Then Redesign?

The findings of the diagnostic team provide the basis for the redesign work that usually follows. But not all companies adhere to this chronology. In some of them, especially when an entire operation is to be changed or when the specific work processes to be reengineered have been identified well in advance, diagnostic and redesign teams work simultaneously. Operating on parallel tracks, one develops a snapshot of the current organization and the other designs a model of its future.

A major advantage to this approach is that it condenses the reengineering timetable considerably. In less than 3 months, an organization can have all the information it needs to conduct a thorough "gap analysis"—assessing how much work has to be done to get from where it is now to where it wants to go—and can quickly begin the process of implementation. But there are also major drawbacks. Operating two teams at once can tie up organizational resources—taking more managers away from their day-to-day functions—and it may reduce the quality of the work these teams produce. When members of the redesign team do not have a solid understanding of the current organization, for example, their designs for the future can sometimes be unrealistic or off-base.

The approach you decide to take will probably depend on the resources you have at your disposal and the time frame in which you have to work. Most companies choose to conduct a diagnosis first and then redesign. In the majority of cases, organizations feel the need to understand exactly what they have to change before they can make decisions with confidence about redesign and implementation.

Notes

1. For more information about the Job Diagnostic Survey, see J. Richard Hackman and Greg R. Oldham, "Development of the Job Diagnostic Survey" *Journal of Applied Psychology*, 60(2). See also J. Richard Hackman, Greg Oldham, Robert Janson, and Kenneth Purdy, "A New Strategy for Job Enrichment," *California Management Review* (Summer 1975): pp. 57–71.

5

Gaining Momentum: Making the Transition from Diagnosis to Redesign

Once an organization has conducted a formal diagnosis, it has reached a critical point in the reengineering process. In most cases, there's no turning back. The work of the diagnostic team has generated so much energy and enthusiasm that many people in the organization are excited about change and anxious to begin the redesign work.

Throughout our experience with organizational change, we have never seen a diagnostic team issue a report that fails to identify significant opportunities for improvement. It simply does not happen. Not once has a team concluded: "We see no reason to change, so we recommend that we continue operating the same way that we have been." On the contrary, whenever a diagnostic team uses the six tools described in Chapter 4, it usually discovers *so many* areas that can be improved that it is difficult for the organization to decide how much redesign work it can realistically handle.

Harnessing and focusing this enthusiasm is the primary challenge in moving from diagnosis to redesign. Ideally, the transition should be a seamless one. The organization should move quickly to select the work process or processes to be redesigned and then set up the team that will do it. No more than 2 or 3 weeks should elapse from the time the diagnostic team presents its findings to the time the redesign team begins its work.

Any significant delay can be detrimental to the change effort. If the break between team activities lasts longer than a month, the organization may fail to capitalize on the energy that diagnosis creates and lose the momentum for change. Just as bad, the information collected by the diagnostic team could lose its relevance, and it may be necessary to repeat some of the data-gathering exercises already conducted.

Rarely do companies decide not to continue at all after completing a diagnosis. But it is possible that a financial crisis or unanticipated change in leadership may force an organization to put its reengineering effort on hold, and in such cases, the impact on the work force can be devastating. The reason is simple: Diagnosis creates strong expectations for change, and when it does not happen, people are disappointed. Like organizations that conduct climate surveys and do not act on the results, those that diagnose without redesigning may do more harm to work force morale than companies that do nothing at all.

Transition Scenarios

The logistics of moving from diagnosis to redesign can vary considerably among organizations that reengineer. Much of it depends on whether the diagnostic team is dissolved after its work is complete, or whether members of the diagnostic team stay on to perform the job of redesign.

The first scenario is most common when an organization has only a vague notion at the start about what work processes it will eventually reengineer. In this situation, what's needed is a diagnostic team with strong data-gathering and analytical skills that can focus solely on providing a comprehensive and objective snapshot of the organization for senior management. From its findings and recommendations, the steering team will select the work processes it believes are in the best interests of the organization to reengineer and then commission a new team to redesign them.

In one midwestern bank, for example, the diagnostic team was charged with examining the organization's entire cash management business: sales, operations, service, and delivery. Among its many findings was the important discovery that the bank lagged behind its competitors in three specific product areas, so the steering team charged a new group with redesigning only those processes that related to the three products.

The second transition scenario—in which members of the diagnostic team stay on to redesign—is most common in organizations where some of the work processes to be reengineered are known before diagnosis, where the areas to be redesigned are narrowly defined, or where the scope of diagnosis and redesign are nearly the same. Here, the diagnostic team can begin to think about what changes to make *while* it's gathering information and data, because it knows that what it's analyzing will also be the subject of future redesign.

In either case, only the steering team can make the final decisions about what the redesign team will actually work on. Although the diagnostic team can make strong recommendations for change—and its proposals are often accepted—it does not have access to all the business and strategic information that is critical to deciding how the reengineering effort should proceed. For example, suppose the diagnostic team wants to introduce an expensive new technology that's being used by some of the organization's competitors. The steering team may decide that an investment of that sort is not feasible because the financial resources simply are not available. Or the diagnostic team may want to redesign a work process that the steering team knows will be phased out once the organization completes its next acquisition.

Three Transition Functions

An important aspect to managing a smooth transition is making good use of the natural break that occurs after the diagnostic team presents its report. In the 2- or 3-week period before redesign work begins, there are three functions you can perform that will strongly enhance the success of your reengineering effort (Figure 5.1).

Review your reengineering strategy. Several months may have gone by since you first decided to reengineer, and given the fast-paced business world we work in today, market conditions may have changed considerably. If so, now is a good time to consider the impact those changes will have on the reengineering

---

1. Review your reengineering strategy.

2. Redefine your success targets.

3. Share your redesign objectives.

FIGURE 5.1. Tasks Between Diagnosis and Redesign

decisions you have made so far: Do you have the same opportunities to achieve change and competitive advantage? Does reengineering still make sense given your new or revised strategic goals? Is reengineering taking you in a direction you still want to go?

Redefine your success targets. Like many organizations that reengineer, you may have begun your change effort with only broad or general objectives—to improve customer service levels, for example, or cut turnaround time. But now that diagnosis has provided new information about what your customers want and what your competitors can deliver, you can establish more specific targets for the redesign work ahead: a 25 percent increase in revenue growth, for example, a 40 percent improvement in order processing time, or an 80 percent reduction in clerical errors. (For details on formulating the redesign objective, see what follows.)

Share your redesign objectives. Communication is a critical element in the transition from diagnosis to redesign, so take the time to share your redesign objectives with others in the organization. This not only validates the contributions they made to the diagnosis, it also raises their level of dissatisfaction with the way things are now and notifies them that major changes are about to take place. Remember: A structured and well-orchestrated communications strategy always helps build participation and commitment by educating employees about reengineering and by helping them anticipate the changes to come.

Formulating the Redesign Objective

What makes a good redesign team target? Only your organization can decide whether a specific objective—like "decrease cycle time by 50 percent"—is appropriate for your reengineering effort. But there are certain characteristics all good targets share that you should consider in *formulating* the more specific target now to be set for redesign. Among them are the following (Figure 5.2):

It's challenging but attainable. Good targets make people reach—often further than they thought they could—and help them to do much more than they ever did before. This "stretch factor" is part of the productive power of targets: It not only sets a goal, it guarantees that people will have to break new

- It's challenging but attainable.

- It's stated in quantified terms.

- It's not open-ended.

- It's firm, but not rigid.

- It identifies process boundaries.

- It's stated in writing.

FIGURE 5.2. Characteristics of an Effective Redesign Objective

ground in order to achieve it. How do you know you have formulated a true "stretch target"? When you feel it's attainable, but you do not know exactly how you will get there.

It's stated in quantified terms. Whatever improvement you are hoping to achieve, you should be able to measure it by calculating or counting something—fewer dollars spent on overhead, for example, or more customers serviced every day or week. Even goals that may seem unquantifiable—like "boosting customer satisfaction"—can be measured *in*directly (by evaluating responses to customer surveys or questionnaires, for example).

It's not open-ended. Adding a time constraint to targets—for example: reducing customer complaints in new policy issues by 75 percent in no more than 18 months—takes them out of the realm of pie-in-the-sky thinking and brings them down to earth. What's more, by committing the team to a schedule of measurement, time limits add a sense of urgency to the redesign work and help the team to focus its efforts even more sharply.

It's firm, but not rigid. It's easier to hit a target that never moves, so your chances of success are enhanced if you maintain the same redesign target throughout your reengineering effort. Remember: A target should be something you feel your organization *ought* to accomplish—regardless of what happens from day to day—so it should not change with the prevailing winds. Still, nothing in the business world these days can be written in stone, so it may be necessary to modify your target as you go along to reflect sudden shifts in market conditions or changes in customer tastes.

It identifies process boundaries. A clear and complete description of what's included in the work processes to be improved will help the team determine the scope of the redesign project. This may not be easy to do; work processes are often involved in a complex maze of interactive or sequential processes and subprocesses, and beginning and end boundaries are sometimes difficult to establish. Nevertheless, it's the only way to identify the departments or functions affected by the redesign, focus everyone's energies in the same direction, and ensure that the redesign work will be manageable.

It's stated in writing. An uncommunicated target has no motivating power. Only when people fully understand what they are supposed to do will they feel compelled to work toward a goal and make the effort to achieve it. Another benefit to putting your objective in writing is that it defines the target more clearly. Writing is more precise than speech, so putting your redesign objective on paper usually ensures that you will not leave anything out.

The Redesign Team

Even when an organization opts for the two-team approach to diagnosis and redesign, we often recommend that some of the same members serve on both teams. It's not a good idea to disband one team and form a completely new one; the success of the redesign team is based so strongly on the results of diagnosis that it always helps when the two teams have some members in common.

Still, many organizations may have to make adjustments in team membership even when they use the single-team approach. Participation on either team can sometimes be so demanding or time-consuming that members may "burn out" from the team experience or face problems coordinating teamwork with their regular job responsibilities. It should come as no surprise, then, if some members of the diagnostic team decide not to work on redesign or if candidates for team membership choose to work on one team and not the other.

The Skills of the Redesign Team

The functional distinction between diagnosis and redesign has led some experts to claim that members of these teams must demonstrate different skills. Diagnosis, they say, is essentially a "left-brain" activity—requiring good planning, organization, and analytical skills—whereas the more "right-brain" activity of redesign requires the ability to synthesize and be creative.

Our experience has shown that those who serve successfully on *either* team are the ones who possess a healthy combination of both skill sets. And this is especially true, we believe, for redesign team members. Although original thinking and a fertile imagination are certainly helpful to redesign, those who are charged with coming up with new ways of working also must be able to determine the feasibility of their concepts, evaluate costs and benefits, and present a thorough case for the ones they recommend for implementation.

Both diagnostic and redesign teams succeed better, of course, when their members possess good interpersonal and communication skills. Although redesign work may require fewer interactions between members of the team and other people in the organization, the intensity and closeness between team members that this type of work entails makes these skills just as critical.

It occasionally happens that a redesign team member will have to be replaced for not showing up for meetings, for example, or failing to participate in other team activities. But rarely are team members discharged from their duties for lacking the right skills. This is because most organizations that reengineer have the good sense to recruit for team membership only their hardest-working and most talented people (Figure 5.3). They know that redesign work is not a job for newcomers or second-stringers, and it never

---

- Possesses good planning, organization, and analytical skills.

- Is able to synthesize and be creative.

- Demonstrates original thinking and a fertile imagination.

- Can evaluate costs and benefits.

- Practices good interpersonal and communication skills.

FIGURE 5.3. Profile of a Redesign Team Member

should be viewed as a testing ground or as an opportunity to build the skills that team members should already possess.

The Size of the Redesign Team

Though diagnostic teams may include as many as 25 members, redesign teams are typically much smaller. Unlike diagnosis, an activity-intensive process that requires many man-hours and plenty of legwork, redesign involves more focused, "in the room" work, so it benefits from limited membership.

Many organizations now commission for redesign a team that consists of a core group of seven or eight members—who work close to full-time—and an outside circle of part-time advisors, consultants, and experts (Figure 5.4). The core group brainstorms process improvements, generates new work designs, and weighs the advantages and disadvantages of different models. Then it contacts members of the outside circle whenever it needs more information, advice, or feedback.

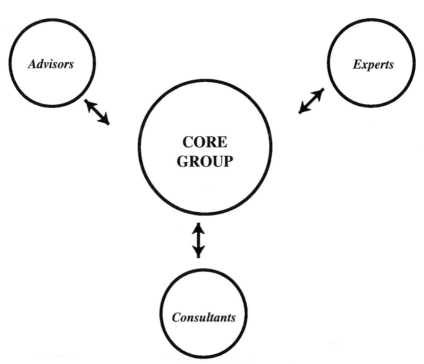

FIGURE 5.4. Components of a Redesign Team

Selecting Redesign Advisors

Those who serve as redesign advisors should be chosen both for their accessibility and for the expertise they can offer to core members of the redesign team. How many should be selected? In theory, members of the core group should be able to call on as many advisors as they feel are necessary to carry out their charge. But to maintain team cohesiveness, most organizations limit the size of the outside circle to between 10 and 20 members.

In selecting redesign team advisors, candidates from any function, department, or level in the organization can be considered (Figure 5.5). We recommend developing an extensive list of possible candidates and then narrowing the selection through a testing process. What follows is a description of candidates commonly considered for membership in the redesign team's outside circle, with the possible advantages and disadvantages listed for each type of candidate.

SUBORDINATES IN LEADERSHIP POSITIONS

Advantages. They are usually familiar with the work processes being redesigned and feel responsible for successfully executing the activities and tasks that make them up. What's more, many want to get ahead and will take advantage of an opportunity to prove themselves, so you can count on them to participate actively in team functions.

- Subordinates in leadership positions.

- Subordinates in production and technical positions.

- Corporate executives.

- Staff specialists.

- Department heads or managers.

- Members of customer teams.

FIGURE 5.5. Candidates for Redesign Team Advisors

Disadvantages. They may have played a role in shaping the current work flow of the processes being redesigned and could be defensive about changing them.

SUBORDINATES IN PRODUCTION AND TECHNICAL POSITIONS

Advantages. They are intimately familiar with the work on a day-to-day basis, may have ideas for improvement that have not been heard yet, and in some cases have extensive knowledge of customers.

Disadvantages. They may be reluctant to voice their opinions in the presence of outsiders or "higher-ups," may defend the status quo, or may have lost the desire to suggest improvements because they harbor negative "we/they" feelings about management.

CORPORATE EXECUTIVES

Advantages. They can add perspective to the team's efforts by counseling members on how their work fits into the "big picture," add information on long-range plans, or facilitate cooperation among the departments involved. They may also include managers who will ultimately review the proposed changes, so selecting them as advisors now may improve the chances of a successful implementation.

Disadvantages. They may not be familiar with the intricacies of the work processes involved, they may be too busy to devote attention to the project, or their participation may inhibit team members from lower levels. They may also try (consciously or otherwise) to gain leadership of the team or exert undue influence.

STAFF SPECIALISTS

Advantages. They may have special knowledge or skills that can help the team identify solutions it has not considered yet or provide guidance in specialized areas, such as teamwork and conflict management (human resources experts), measurement and design (engineers), financial and legal matters (accountants and lawyers), or technology (systems analysts).

Disadvantages. As "outsiders" to the work processes involved, they may not be trusted by members of the core group or might be suspected of promoting hidden agendas.

DEPARTMENT HEADS OR MANAGERS

Advantages. They may have access to important information—figures on labor, overhead, or materials costs, for example—that could be critical to the team's understanding of the processes being worked on. They also have the power to promote the team's ideas and recommendations within their departments.

Disadvantages. They may oppose any changes that could undermine their authority or use their position to encourage active resistance to the team's redesign recommendations.

MEMBERS OF CUSTOMER TEAMS

Advantages. They may have an intimate knowledge of the needs and expectations of your customers and are in the best position to predict what customers will want in the future. They may also possess a wealth of creative ideas on how things need to change in order to "delight" customers or exceed their requirements.

Disadvantages. Their suggestions may be unrealistic. Because they focus so strongly on improving customer satisfaction, they often fail to take into consideration organizational or resource limitations.

Timetable for Redesign

Although redesign work is in no way any less important than diagnosis, it usually takes far less time (Figure 5.6). Exactly how much time you need to redesign will depend on the size of your organization and the scope of your reengineering effort. But if it takes you 7 or 8 weeks to complete a comprehensive diagnosis, say, you can probably finish most of your redesign work in less than 5 weeks.

This is possible because of the way redesign work is usually carried out—in 1- or 2-day sessions that are held by the core group every week or every other week. Because a lot of creativity and mental concentration is required for redesign, it helps when the team can meet for eight or more hours at a stretch and work without disruption. Then the team members can use the time between meetings to replenish their creative juices or bounce ideas off members of the outer circle.

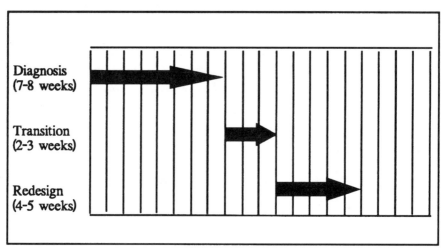

FIGURE 5.6.   Diagnosis/Redesign Timetable

It's surprising how much work can be accomplished in just a few redesign sessions. One company, for example, made change a top priority and decided to commission a team to work full-time on redesign. Given carte blanche to call on any member of the organization for help or advice, the team was able to present the blueprint for a complete organizational transformation in just 6 weeks—redesigning one work process, on average, every week and a half!

The Pitfalls of Redesign

Like diagnosis—which can sometimes degenerate into mere number crunching or slip into "analysis paralysis"—redesign work has its potential dangers. So the steering team and the reengineering coordinator should continually monitor team activities to make sure that the redesign work remains solidly on track. There are four pitfalls they should specifically watch for (Figure 5.7).

Loss of focus. Redesign team members may become so excited by the many possibilities for change that they lose sight of the targets established by the steering team or waste time pursuing ideas outside the scope and parameters of the reengineering effort. Without the discipline required to focus on the issues that fall within their charge, team members can be easily distracted by information on what competitors are doing or by fancy new technologies, even though these approaches may be impractical for your organization or irrelevant to the work processes being redesigned.

- Loss of focus.

- All-or-nothing mentality.

- Ivory-tower syndrome.

- Home-run mentality.

FIGURE 5.7.   Pitfalls of Redesign

All-or-nothing mentality. Redesign team members may spend all their time developing the one best design that they feel will solve your organization's problems. But when it's criticized by others—or rejected as undoable—they can easily become frustrated or demoralized. That's why team members should not be encouraged to invest all their energy into only one concept and try to come up with a variety of options. A strategy they can use to accomplish this is to form subgroups within the team, and charge each subgroup with creating its own redesign concept.

Ivory-tower syndrome. Redesign team members may become so absorbed in the creative, idea-generating aspects of their work that they begin to isolate themselves from those outside the team's core group and fail to seek input from others in the organization. Without the continuous feedback they need to give their work perspective, however, they may devote large amounts of time and energy to ideas that will ultimately prove unworkable or become emotionally attached to redesign concepts that others may dislike. It's important to remind team members that the ideas they come up with are always "works in progress" and that they are bound to improve when the suggestions of others are taken into account.

Home-run mentality. Redesign team members may become so enamored of big or complicated solutions that they overlook the obvious possibilities for improvement or miss opportunities for change that are quickly and easily implemented. Sometimes the introduction of a simple checklist, for example, or the elimination of a routine report can make a substantial difference in workplace productivity. But the redesign team is unlikely to recognize these opportunities if it's focusing solely on concepts that involve massive or sweeping change.

One bank, for example, was so concerned about checks being inadvertently thrown out that it used to bag its trash daily, tag it, and send it to a warehouse for storage. When the company reengineered, its redesign team recommended that this practice be discontinued because it was clearly not cost-effective. In the previous 5 years, the team found, only one check had ever been lost—and it could not be found in the stored trash!

How can you develop a redesign team that's capable of hitting "singles" as well as "home runs"? Make sure team members are aware that changes that seem to have nothing to do with reengineering per se—that do not redesign jobs, for example, or fail to alter the structure of the organization—can still make a difference to quality, productivity, and profitability, and that substantial benefits can be gained from the accumulation of small quick improvements.

6

The Redesign Process—Part I: Generating New Process Concepts

Many organizations approach the redesign phase of reengineering with apprehensions and fears. Typically, they have two concerns. One is that it is too risky, because redesign relies so much on the results produced by a single team. The other is that it is too haphazard or unpredictable, because redesign is essentially a creative process that cannot be managed or controlled.

Our experience shows that these fears are generally unwarranted. Although reengineering is not risk-free—in many cases, in fact, the entire future of an organization rests on what its reengineering effort can achieve—companies sometimes expose themselves to much greater dangers these days by making no changes. What's more, the risk associated with reengineering isn't necessarily generated during the redesign phase. When a company has conducted the preliminary work described in this book and completed a comprehensive diagnosis, the members of the redesign team and those who work with it usually have a better knowledge of their organization and its customers than they have ever had before, fully understand the consequences of *not* changing, and are strongly motivated to succeed. For these reasons, redesign work is usually carried out smoothly and efficiently, and the reforms proposed as a result of it almost always provide significant organizational benefits (Fig. 6.1).

Apprehensions related to the creative aspects of redesign are also based on misunderstandings. Naturally, any company would have reservations about giving one small team the authority to modify organizational structure as much as it wanted to or totally reinvent work processes from scratch. But that

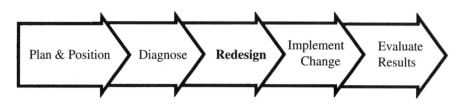

FIGURE 6.1.　The Five Phases of Reengineering

is not a completely accurate description of what a redesign team does. Although brainstorming, "out-of-the-box" thinking, and other idea-generating exercises are an important part of the redesign process, the team must also rigorously assess whatever new concepts it comes up with and evaluate them for their compatibility with strategic goals, their cost-effectiveness, and the likelihood that they can be implemented.

It is not true that redesign is a haphazard or unmanageable process. On the contrary, successful redesign teams follow a well-structured methodology that helps to guide them from the idea-generating stage of redesign through the subsequent stages of analysis and implementation. This chapter and the two that follow describe this methodology in detail and take you through the steps that are likely to result in successful redesign.

In this chapter, you will learn how the team accomplishes the first stage of redesign, generating new process "concepts"—those work designs that can potentially replace, and dramatically improve on, the existing work process. There are three critical steps involved in this stage:

1. "Blank slating" the future.

2. Brainstorming multiple options.

3. Selecting the best option.

"Blank Slating" the Future

Much of what is learned in diagnosing the organization will be useful in helping the redesign team determine the benefits and drawbacks of new work designs, establish their feasibility, and select the best options for implementation. But before the team can get to that point, its members first will have to generate some truly innovative design concepts, and the best way for them to do that is to start practicing what creativity experts call "blank slating" the future—that is, to free themselves of the limitations and restrictions of work processes as they exist and to open their minds to totally new possibilities.

There are three blank-slating techniques that will prepare the redesign team to brainstorm new design concepts (see Figure 6.2). Each technique will help start the creative juices flowing, encourage thinking that's original and imaginative, and facilitate the team's efforts at developing multiple design options.

Begin to think like a customer. One good way for team members to put themselves in the right frame of mind to begin process redesign is to imagine that *they* are the customers of their organization and to ask themselves the types of questions that will help them understand how customers think and feel. Some examples include the following:

- What do I need from this work process?

- What do I expect from this work process?

- What are the qualities or attributes of the process that would truly please or delight me?

It's surprising how many organizations still function on the basis of outmoded concepts of work efficiency, without taking into account what their customers want or need (Figure 6.3). To reengineer successfully, they must perform their redesign work *from the outside in*—first by identifying customer needs and expectations and then by creating the kinds of jobs, work flows, and technical support systems that can fully satisfy those expectations.

How does thinking like a customer lead to new process design possibilities? When team members adopt the customer's viewpoint, they begin to

---

- Begin to think like a customer.

- Review existing benchmark data.

- Apply common rules of creativity.

FIGURE 6.2. Step 1: "Blank Slate" the Future

- Quality
- Variety
- Convenience
- Promptness
- Affordability
- Accuracy
- Courtesy
- Reliability

- Honesty
- Efficiency
- One-stop service
- Customization
- Add-on value
- High-tech
- High-touch

FIGURE 6.3. Customer Demands

focus less on the details and mechanics of the process and more on its ultimate *purpose*—the value and benefits that it creates for customers. And that simple shift in perspective often frees them to imagine new ways of organizing or performing work.

One example of an organization that is initiating radical change in its work systems by adopting a stronger customer orientation is the U.S. Postal Service. Its "store of the future" concept, which will become the standard design for all new post offices and renovations, stresses convenience over efficiency by introducing self-service stations that allow customers to weigh packages, buy postage, and get a receipt without ever having to wait at a full-service counter.[1]

To help members get the most from this technique, the redesign team may want to invite one or more members of a customer team to sit in on its brainstorming sessions or to include other people in the organization who are considered good "listening posts" for customer information (such as sales, marketing, or service people).

Review existing benchmark data. Another technique that helps team members think more creatively is benchmarking: comparing work processes to those that are similar in competitive organizations, in world-class organizations, or in other parts of the same organization. Benchmarking is carried out in the diagnostic phase to help identify which work processes should be redesigned, but here it serves a different purpose—to provide inspiration for new design concepts or to establish work models the redesign team can adapt or improve on.

Rarely can the design of a work process be transported in its entirety from one organization to another—even when both operate in the same industry—because of differences in culture, management style, or work force makeup. But simply knowing that there are other ways to make a product, provide a service, or execute a clerical function can help members of the redesign team break free of traditional work concepts and begin to envision new design possibilities.

Benchmarking with organizations in unrelated industries (sometimes called "best practices") is especially conducive to breakthrough thinking. The reason: Seeing how customers are being satisfied in totally different businesses can be a mind-expanding experience that sometimes leads to fresh insights to old problems and new ideas on how to organize work. Many banks, for example, are now beginning to look at fast-food operations for tips on how to provide multiple products with ease and convenience. As a result, some are beginning to add mutual-fund transactions to the list of functions on their ATMs, for example, or they are bundling their products as "value packages" that tie together checking, savings, and credit services for a flat monthly fee.[2]

Apply common rules of creativity. The redesign team will not succeed at developing new work designs unless it creates the proper environment for brainstorming, one in which members feel free enough to say what they think, are not afraid of being criticized or judged, and do not worry about making mistakes. The faster the team can develop this open and supportive environment, the sooner its members will overcome their inhibitions, take creative risks, and work together to generate new ideas.

Here are 10 standard rules that help promote a comfortable and creative team environment.

1. Constantly ask the two key questions that foster creativity the most: *Why?* and *What if?*

2. Focus on finding good answers and solutions—not on finding the one "right" answer.

3. Avoid premature decision making or closure.

4. Give everyone the opportunity to explain his or her views and to respond to the ideas of others.

5. Avoid behavior that blocks creative thinking, such as name calling, stereotyping, or looking at problems from only one perspective.

6. Withhold comments and criticisms until after meetings or until everyone's ideas have been presented.

7. Do not rely solely on logical or rational thinking, which can overlook seemingly impractical or implausible solutions.

8. Acknowledge the legitimacy of feelings by encouraging team members to discuss their reactions and emotions.

9. Avoid the kinds of comments that inhibit people from expressing their views and opinions, such as

"That will never work here."

"We tried that before."

"Senior management will never approve it."

"It would be too expensive or too much trouble."

10. Don't be overly serious. Playfulness contributes to creativity and often helps generate constructive ideas.[3]

Brainstorming Multiple Options

In time, the redesign team will come up with a detailed description of a new process design that it will recommend as a replacement for the existing one. But, first, team members will have to work closely with each other to brainstorm a number of redesign options (Figure 6.4).

The primary objective of brainstorming is to generate as many new ideas as possible—no matter how crude or implausible—without critical evaluation. The reason for this approach is that research has shown that creativity feeds

---

- Challenge basic assumptions.

- Rethink process attributes.

- Apply reengineering principles.

- Follow redesign guidelines.

FIGURE 6.4.   Step 2: Brainstorm Multiple Options

on itself. The *more* ideas a team generates, the *better* its ideas become. And even ideas that are bizarre or outlandish may contain elements that could later be integrated into a workable design, or that provide the mental bridge leading to other valuable—and more feasible—process concepts.

There are three brainstorming techniques that can help the redesign team generate a multitude of ideas for new work process concepts.

Challenge basic assumptions. Management consultant Michael Hammer says that successful reengineering requires radically new ideas—what he calls "out-of-the-box" thinking—and one of the best ways to generate those ideas is by examining the fundamental assumptions about the existing work process or the basic principles by which the organization operates. Once these assumptions and principles are brought to light, says Hammer, they may be found to be no longer true or applicable, and that can undermine the rationale for traditional ways of working.

When one progressive supermarket in the Netherlands decided to improve its basic service, for example, it began to question the very notion that employees must be present to charge customers for what they buy. Now, armed with portable, hand-held scanners that record each item as it's taken from the shelf, store shoppers can bag their purchases as they move along and spend far less time waiting in checkout lines. When they return their equipment to the scanner station, they receive a full bill printout in just a matter of seconds.[4]

Asking questions like the ones that follow will help the redesign team to uncover underlying assumptions, determine their value and continued relevance, and imagine new possibilities for how work can be organized or performed.

- What benefits do customers receive from this process, and are these the benefits customers are still looking for? Have our customers developed new needs or expectations that this process currently does not meet?

- How many people perform this work and what kinds of skills does it require? What would happen if the process were performed by people with different skills and abilities? What if we had only half the number of people to do the work?

- Why are the tasks and activities that make up this process performed in this order or sequence? What would happen if the order were changed? What would happen if some of the activities were eliminated?

- How much time do people have to complete the process, and how was that time calculated? What if we had only half the time to complete the process?

Another way to practice out-of-the-box thinking is by examining a flow chart of the existing process and then posing questions around new possibilities for arranging tasks and activities, directing the flow of work, or assigning work responsibilities. Some examples follow:

- What if we had to cut the number of subprocesses in half?

- What if we reorder the tasks and activities?

- What if we combine two independent subprocesses?

- At what different points could the customer be involved in the process?

- What if we eliminated authorizations and checkpoints?

- What if the people needed to complete the process were all located in the same department or unit?

Rethink process characteristics. Another good way to stimulate thinking about work design possibilities is to identify the principal characteristics that describe a given process and then consider how the process would operate if a particular characteristic were eliminated or changed.

It's a good idea to group the characteristics into general categories—like technology, information, and people—and then try to generate as many new ideas as possible around each category. Here are some examples:

- *Technology:* What would happen if . . .

  — all repetitive tasks and activities were automated?

  — the technology could be operated by anyone?

  — routine decisions were translated into computer protocols?

  — the same document could be accessed at different sites simultaneously?

  — the customer was linked to the same computer system?

- *Information:* What would happen if . . .

  — customer data were accessible to all employees?

  — information was easier to understand and interpret?

  — customer data were collected only once?

  — no information had to be rekeyed or reentered?

  — all information systems were integrated?

- *People:* What would happen if . . .

  — those who performed it were better trained?

  — those who performed it were empowered to make more decisions?

  — those who performed it possessed multiple skills?

  — those who performed it were located in the same area?

  — those who performed it had better interpersonal or communication skills?

Morris Air, a low-cost airline based in Salt Lake City, went through a similar creative process recently when it revamped its reservation system by asking: How could we improve our service if we didn't issue tickets? Now travelers who book flights directly with the airline simply give their credit card number over the phone when they book a flight and only have to show identification at the gate in order to walk on board. By banishing tickets—some 12,000 a day—the company saves time and money and doesn't have to refund lost documents or field complaints from customers whose tickets haven't arrived.[5]

Apply reengineering principles. Whenever the redesign team encounters roadblocks during its brainstorming activities or falls into a creativity slump, it helps to remember the ultimate purpose of reengineering: to bring about positive changes in the effectiveness and efficiency of work processes and to improve responsiveness to customers. Reviewing the five basic principles of reengineering may also recharge the group's creative powers and keep its thinking on the right track. The five reengineering principles are as follows:

1. *Make the customer the starting point for change.* Companies that reengineer focus first on what their customers want—speed, variety, or one-stop service, for example—and then make the kinds of changes that will help to satisfy customers. In many cases, these changes result in work teams that are strongly customer-focused and in jobs that increase feelings of accountability and ownership.

To apply this principle as they brainstorm, team members should ask the following:

- Is the existing process designed around archaic principles of work efficiency and management control?

- Is there another way we can organize ourselves that would promote a stronger customer focus?

- How can we restructure to increase our flexibility and responsiveness to customers?

2. *Design work processes in light of organizational goals.* To achieve higher levels of quality, productivity, and customer service, many companies that reengineer reconfigure existing jobs by combining work procedures or tasks, creating "natural" work units, or establishing more effective feedback channels. These changes usually lead to more positive customer attitudes and better service delivery, work that's more interesting and challenging for employees, and a stronger sense of job ownership.

To apply this principle as they brainstorm, team members should ask the following:

- How many jobs are required to complete this process, and which ones can be combined?

- Does each job have a natural beginning and end; how can we transform "incomplete" jobs into "whole" ones?

- What structural barriers limit a worker's access to feedback from customers, supervisors, or co-workers?

3. *Reorganize to support front-line performance.* Many companies that reengineer establish multiskilled teams to support their customer service people, or they use advanced technologies to create "workstation professionals" who can

service customers completely by performing both front- and back-office functions. These changes usually foster stronger feelings of professionalism among workers, reduce the need for close supervision or monitoring, and promote more efficient service delivery.

To apply this principle as they brainstorm, team members should ask the following:

- How does the division of work hinder work efficiency or interfere with service delivery?

- How can we redesign the work process to promote feelings of ownership and accountability?

- How can we use technology to improve our people's ability to service customers and get things done?

4. *Empower employees to make decisions in favor of the customer.* Many companies that reengineer redesign jobs so that front-line workers are more responsible for satisfying customers, can make customer-related decisions more quickly, or can rely on "expert" systems for information and guidance in serving customers. Changes like these usually increase feelings of accountability and the commitment to quality, and allow workers to make the kinds of decisions that once required the input of managers.

To apply this principle as they brainstorm, team members should ask the following:

- Does the design of the work promote feelings of responsibility at the lowest levels?

- Do existing jobs stifle initiative and dampen creativity, and are authorization levels too high?

- Does our use of technology help to empower our people?

5. *Partner with the customer in a long-term relationship.* Many companies that reengineer establish teams that face off against a specific geographic region or market segment and that eliminate multiple points of customer contact by providing a complete range of services to customers. Changes like these build stronger relationships with customers, promote the principle of one-stop service, and help employees better understand customer needs.

To apply this principle as they brainstorm, team members should ask the following:

- Does the current structure of the process foster strong relationships with customers?

- How can we redesign to increase the quantity and quality of our customer contacts?

- How can we automate tasks and procedures to free up workers and allow them to spend more time with customers or to work on more important activities?

Follow redesign guidelines. Like any improvement strategy, reengineering works best when it's tailored to your specific environment—the culture you work in and the customers you serve. But there are redesign guidelines that can be followed in just about every reengineering situation to make work more efficient, improve service quality, and increase commitment and job satisfaction (Figure 6.5). These guidelines include the following.

Flatten the hierarchy. You can eliminate the need for excessive layers of management—and increase feelings of ownership and accountability—by redesigning your organization to simplify its structure. In many cases, this means relying more on self-managed work teams that need little supervision or on those employees whose skills and knowledge have been increased.

As the redesign team brainstorms, it should ask the following:

- How many layers of management do we now have supervising this work process, and how many do we really need?

- How can we restructure to create a leaner and more flexible work process?

Eliminate unnecessary work. You can shorten the time it takes to complete the work process by streamlining tasks and activities and trimming excess or wasted effort. This often means eliminating multiple approvals and checkpoints, error proofing activities to avoid rework, or automating boring and routine tasks.

As the redesign team brainstorms, it should ask the following:

1. Flatten the hierarchy.

2. Eliminate unnecessary work.

3. Create multiskilled jobs.

4. Rely on teams.

5. Integrate parallel processing activities.

6. Create a storehouse of customer information.

FIGURE 6.5.   Guidelines for Redesign

- What is the real value added by each task or activity performed, and how does it contribute to satisfying customer needs or requirements?

- Is any of the work irrelevant or redundant?

Create multiskilled jobs. You can improve job satisfaction and customer service by redesigning jobs so that they integrate a multitude of tasks and procedures and require a variety of skills. This usually means training employees to complete all or many of the tasks it takes to service a particular group of customers or to produce a single product or service.

As the redesign team brainstorms, it should ask the following:

- How many of the tasks involved in this work process can be performed by the same person?

- How many jobs are required to complete the process and which ones can be combined?

Rely on teams. Teams are a common component of reengineering because they are the chief mechanism many organizations use to deliver one-stop service. What kinds of teams work best to raise service levels? More and more companies are relying on self-directed or self-managed teams, whose members are well trained and who together possess all the skills needed to complete the work process.

As the redesign team brainstorms, it should ask the following:

- Can we set up work teams or service teams that eliminate the need for handoffs or transfers?

- What kinds of skills or training do our people need to work independently on teams?

Integrate parallel processing activities. You can save time, reduce the need for rework, and improve service delivery by coordinating similar activities among separate functions while they are being carried out—rather than after they are completed—or by converting sequential activities into parallel ones. In most cases, this requires computer systems that allow multiple users to tap into the same program or database.

As the redesign team brainstorms, it should ask the following:

- Does our use of personal computers, local-area networks, and on-line systems allow us to enter or retrieve data from any location?

- Does our use of technology promote the principle of one-stop service?

Create a storehouse of customer information. To lower overhead costs and reduce the possibility of multiple-entry errors, make sure that important customer information is collected once—by the person who knows the customer best—and that it's stored in a database that can be shared by other parts of your organization. This eliminates unnecessary information exchanges and the need for each unit or team to create its own customer profile.

As the redesign team brainstorms, it should ask the following:

- Can we create a customer database to which everyone has access?

- Does our use of technology give workers access to the critical information they need to service customers quickly and efficiently?

Selecting the Best Option

Chances are the brainstorming activities just described will help the redesign team members to generate a number of good ideas, and they will probably come up with several new design concepts—each representing an improvement over the existing work process. How will team members know which design offers the greatest potential for achieving breakthroughs in productivity, quality, and customer satisfaction? They will have to carefully weigh the advantages and disadvantages of each option to select the best one.[6] There are several ways to do this (Figure 6.6).

Measure against reengineering parameters and success targets. One basic question must be asked first in any preliminary evaluation of design options: Does the new design concept fall within the defined scope and parameters of your reengineering effort (see Chapter 3) and does it meet your established success targets?

If clear process boundaries were established at the start, for example, then the redesign team can eliminate those options that fail to cover all the activities, functions, or departments that were initially included as part of the process definition. If your reengineering timetable has been firmly set at 18 months, then the team can eliminate those options that will probably take longer to implement. Or if you initially decided that the redesigned process should reduce cycle time by 50 percent, then the team can eliminate those options that are unlikely to achieve this result.

A simple chart (see Figure 6.7) can help the team to identify which redesign options are both consistent with the scope and parameters of the change effort and meet its success targets.

Apply C.E.O. thinking to assess benefits. Another way to compare new design options is to determine how well and in what ways they would benefit the

---

1. Measure against reengineering parameters and success targets.

2. Apply C.E.O. thinking to assess benefits.

3. Develop structure and infrastructure details.

4. Develop a concept evaluation matrix.

FIGURE 6.6. Step 3: Select the Best Option

	Falls within scope and parameters	Meets defined success targets
Concept 1:	✓	
Concept 2:	✓	✓
Concept 3:		✓
Concept 4:	✓	✓
Concept 5:		
Concept 6:		✓

FIGURE 6.7. A Simple Option Chart

three most important stakeholders of the work process: your customers, your employees, and your organization. To apply C.E.O. thinking to process concept comparisons, the redesign team should ask a series of questions for each of the three stakeholders:

To determine customer benefits, the team should ask the following:

- How well does the design concept improve accuracy and reliability?

- What effect will the design concept have on turnaround time or responsiveness to customers?

- How much will the design concept improve product or service quality?

- How well will the design concept meet customer requirements—or exceed them?

- Does the design concept improve our ability to monitor customer satisfaction?

To determine employee benefits, the team should ask the following:

- What impact will the design concept have on job variety and job satisfaction?

- Does the design concept eliminate unnecessary work steps and tedious or mundane tasks?

- Does the design concept provide timely and effective feedback on job performance?

- Does the design concept create "whole" jobs that enhance feelings of job ownership?

- Does the design concept empower workers and provide opportunities for them to use their judgment, make decisions, and exercise authority?

To determine organizational benefits, the team should ask the following:

- How effective is the design concept at reducing operating costs (labor, materials, overhead, etc.)?

- What impact will the design concept have on productivity and profitability?

- How much will the design concept contribute to helping the organization achieve its business or strategic goals?

- How much does the design concept contribute to increasing the organization's competitiveness?

- How does the design concept help the organization anticipate customer needs or respond better to shifting markets?

Develop structure and infrastructure details. Any comparison of new process design concepts should also include a thorough evaluation of the details and features that characterize each option. That means the redesign team should consider not only the impact each concept will have on the *structure* of the work process—like work flow, technology, and elapsed work time—it should also consider whatever repercussions the design will have on the process *infrastructure*—like training requirements, management style, and compensation. Focusing on the structure and infrastructure details will give the team a good idea of the immediate benefits and drawbacks of each option, and it will provide a more complete picture of what it will take to *sustain* each new work design over the long term.

To conduct this exercise, the redesign team may want to construct a large table on a chalkboard or flipchart that allows comparisons of the structure and infrastructure details for each new design option. (The team can use Figure 6.8 as a model, although it may want to add more cells or make some cells larger to accommodate fuller descriptions.)

Develop a concept evaluation matrix. Finally, the redesign team members can compare the new design concepts they have come up with to each other—and to the existing work process—by using a tool called a *concept evaluation matrix* (Figure 6.9).[7] This tool can help the team to rank the new designs, consider trade-offs among them, and then select the best candidate for analysis and implementation. Here's how it works.

A concept evaluation matrix establishes the existing work process as a baseline against which each new design concept can be qualitatively measured. Along the left side of the matrix are listed all the criteria that the team members have agreed are the most important to the change effort: reliability, accuracy, ratio of real work time to elapsed time, efficiency, reduced costs, number of handoffs, number of workers involved, whatever. Along the top of the matrix are listed the design concepts proposed.

	Concept 1	Concept 2	Concept 3	Concept 4	Concept 5	Concept 6
Work flow						
Technology						
Elapsed time						
Other						
Other						
Management style						
Compen-sation						
Training						
Other						
Other						

FIGURE 6.8. Comparing Structure and Infrastructure Details

After the team has created the evaluation matrix, it then rates each design concept on each criterion as it compares to the existing process.

- If the team feels the new design concept is better than the existing process, it marks the chart with a **+**.

- If the team feels the new design concept is not as good as the existing process, it marks the chart with a **−**.

- If the team has any doubts about whether the new design concept is better or worse than the existing process, it marks the chart with an **S.**

Criteria	Concept 1	Concept 2	Concept 3	Concept 4	Concept 5	Concept 6	Concept 7
Total +:							
Total S:							
Total −:							

FIGURE 6.9. Concept Evaluation Matrix

As the team evaluates each concept against each criterion, it may want to brainstorm ideas on how to change a − or an **S** to a +.

The +, −, and **S** scores are for guidance only and should not be added together. But they can provide some indication of which concepts are strongest—and may qualify as candidates for the final selection—and which, conversely, are weakest. As a closing exercise, the team may want to examine the "losing" concepts to determine if it can incorporate some of their +'s into the final selection.

Notes

1. For more information, see "Post Offices Nationwide to Undergo Redesign," *Wall Street Journal*, August 30, 1993, p. B5.

2. See "Banks Court Disenchanged Customers," *Wall Street Journal*, August 30, 1993, p. B5.

3. For more information on how to stimulate playfulness and overcome barriers to creativity, see Roger Von Oech, *Whack on the Side of the Head* (New York: Warner Books, 1983).

4. See "Do-It-Yourself Grocery Checkout," *Wall Street Journal*, January 31, 1994, p. B1.

5. See "The Paperless Society Takes a Leap Forward With a Ticketless Airline," *Wall Street Journal*, October 22, 1993, p. B1.

6. If the team decides that more than one option offers significant promise, it may want to consider two or more options during the next stage of the reengineering process, "Analyzing Candidate Concepts" (see Chapter 7).

7. For more information on the concept evaluation matrix, see Stuart Pugh, *Total Design: Integrated Methods for Successful Product Engineering* (Reading, MA: Addison-Wesley, 1991).

7

The Redesign Process—Part II: Analyzing New Process Concepts

Many people assume that the work devoted to selecting a new process concept completes the redesign phase of reengineering. But that's a mistaken notion. For no matter how creative the new concept the redesign team comes up with, it's job is far from over. Before making a formal proposal for implementation, the team must also conduct a thorough *analysis* of the concept it chooses.

Why bother? Because even when a new concept seems to represent a clear improvement over the process it's intended to replace, its feasibility must still be determined. Changes that look good on paper may not appear so practical or desirable once everything that's involved in executing them is taken into account. Without analyzing a new concept, there's no way for the redesign team to know if it can be easily implemented, for example, what kinds of changeover costs it may entail, or whether it will be readily accepted by others in the organization.

There are three good reasons why the redesign team should conduct a new concept analysis (Figure 7.1):

1. *It helps the team refine the concept.* As the team analyzes the new concept, it will produce a more detailed description of the work design it's proposing and, in the process, may discover aspects of it that can be improved further. These refinements to the new design could result in additional gains in productivity, product quality, or customer service.

2. *It helps identify potential obstacles to implementation.* As the team analyzes the new concept, it will gain a better understanding of what changes will have

1. It gives the redesign team time to refine the concept.

2. It helps the redesign team identify obstacles to implementation.

3. It prepares the redesign team to "sell" the change recommendation.

FIGURE 7.1. Three Reasons for Conducting a New Concept Analysis

to be made to implement the design and make it workable. This increased awareness may lead the team to rethink or modify the design—to make it more compatible with the organization's culture, for example, or more palatable to those who might resist the change.

3. *It helps prepare the team to "sell" the change recommendation.* As the team analyzes the new concept, it will become intimately familiar with every facet of the new design, its benefits and drawbacks, as well as the possible risks involved in implementation. This will help the team to present a clear and convincing proposal for change, develop ways to minimize or overcome design flaws, and prepare for any objections to which the new design may give rise.

Although it does not happen often, it is possible that the redesign team may decide in the end to scrap or shelve a new design. Its analysis may reveal, for example, that a crucial technology the design depends on will be unaffordable or unavailable, that the costs of implementation will substantially exceed original estimates, or that the time it takes employees to learn required new skills will be longer than the organization can realistically wait. In cases like these, the team may select an alternative concept to propose for implementation, or it may return to the drawing board and begin the idea-generating process all over again.

In this chapter, you will learn how the redesign team carries out the second critical stage of redesign (Figure 7.2): analyzing new process concepts. There are four basic steps involved in this stage:

1. Predicting process performance.

2. Identifying real-world roadblocks.

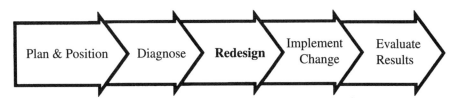

FIGURE 7.2.   The Five Phases of Reengineering

3. Identifying potential quick hits.

4. Preparing to sell the change recommendation.

Predicting Process Performance

Before it's actually up and running, there's no way of knowing for sure whether a new work design will operate significantly better than the existing one or that it will produce the breakthroughs in cycle time, reliability, productivity, or quality that you hope to achieve. Still, it is possible to make a fairly accurate prediction of how the process will perform based on what's already known about your organization (the available human, technological, and financial resources, for example, and your ability to change and adapt) and a detailed flow chart of the proposed design. This flow chart should indicate all the subprocesses, activities, and specific tasks to be completed in the new design, as well as material flows, information flows, and decision points.

With this information at hand, there are two techniques the redesign team can use that will help predict the performance of a new work concept (Figure 7.3).

Estimating requirements. Determining what resources will be required to maintain the proposed work process and to keep it operating smoothly is one

---

1. *Estimate requirements.*

2. *Calculate benefits and costs.*

FIGURE 7.3.   Step 1: Predict Process Performance

way to assess its effectiveness before implementation. There are three basic categories of resource requirements that should be considered (Figure 7.4).

1. *Human resource requirements:* How many employees will be required to staff the new process? What types of employees will be needed (claims processors, technicians, customer service people, managers, etc.)? What skills must they learn to carry out the process? Who will provide any additional training that's required?

HUMAN RESOURCE REQUIREMENTS

- What types of positions?
- How many people?
- Who will provide training?

INFORMATION REQUIREMENTS

- What kinds of data?
- How will they be updated?
- Who will maintain them?

EQUIPMENT REQUIREMENTS

- What kinds of technology?
- How many new machines?
- Who will install them?

FIGURE 7.4.   Requirements for Predicting Process Performance

2. *Information requirements:* What types of data or information will employees need access to in order to complete the process? How frequently will this data have to be collected? Who will be charged with maintaining or updating these data? What kinds of systems will be required to store the data?

3. *Equipment requirements:* What kinds of computer technologies (PCs, local-area networks, on-line systems, etc.) must be purchased or set up to facilitate the new process? Will "smart" or "expert" systems be used to automate activities, and who will install them? How many and what types of copiers, faxes, telephones, or other types of office machines will be needed?

The redesign team may also want to consider *physical plant* requirements for the new process (office space, heating, and air conditioning, for example) and *supplier* requirements, if they differ significantly from those for the existing process.

Calculating benefits and costs. Once the redesign team has determined the requirements—or "inputs"—for the new process, it should then try to analyze the probable results of the process: its "outcomes." After all, you cannot determine if an idea is worth implementing simply by deciding whether or not it "sounds good"; you must try to predict its impact or what it will actually produce.

The two most important outcomes to be considered during any thorough analysis are *benefits* and *costs*, and these should be stated as quantitatively as possible (Figure 7.5). Using numbers to analyze a new work concept has a significant and positive side effect: It permits measurement of the new idea. If you can predict the results of a proposed work design and compare them to the results of the existing process, then your comparison will serve as a reliable measure of the value of your proposal.

Benefits. When the team calculates the benefits of the proposed design, it should always measure improvements in productivity, cycle time (processing time plus any waiting and transporting time), and defect rates, as well as the financial returns expected from these two sources:

1. *Cost savings.* These include all the savings incurred from increased work efficiencies, from reduced defects, or from better quality and improved reliability.

Benefits

- Improved productivity
- Reduced cycle time
- Fewer defect rates
- Cost savings
- Increased revenues

Costs

- Higher operating costs
- Added personnel
- New equipment
- Lost work time
- Consultant fees and technical assistance

FIGURE 7.5. Calculations for Predicting Process Performance

(One example of a company that has reaped substantial cost savings through reengineering is Huntington Bancshares of Columbus, Ohio, which developed a sophisticated electronic-banking system that includes a 24-hour telephone service, video phones for processing loans and opening accounts, and a pay-by-phone option that responds to spoken instructions. Although the bank has invested $25 million in the new system, it projects huge savings in operating expenses because 40 percent of all transactions will now be handled by phone.[1])

2. *Increased revenues.* These include the additional revenues expected from increased market share, from new sales, or from the prevention of lost sales.

(Self-service gas stations that allow drivers to pay by credit card directly at the pump are good examples of how process redesign can increase sales and revenues. The initial costs of installing these machines has been estimated at a hefty $15,000 per pump, but surveys show that gasoline sales typically rise

5 percent or more after card readers are installed, and it's not uncommon for sales of soda, cigarettes, and snacks also to go up.[2])

Costs. When the team calculates the costs of the proposed design, it should always estimate operating costs (direct labor, material, and overhead costs), the total cost of the implementation, *plus* any new costs associated with maintaining the process, such as the following:

- hiring new employees

- training existing employees

- purchasing new equipment or technology

- moving to new facilities

- lost work time

- hiring consultants or technical experts

- designing new information systems.

Obviously, any analysis of the benefits and costs of a new work concept cannot be made with total precision. The implementation of the design may take longer than expected, new technologies may not work as anticipated, or the design may create problems that cannot be foreseen. For these reasons, it's a good idea to calculate "best case" and "worst case" benefit-and-cost estimates. What's involved? First, calculate the results you can expect when the implementation goes as smoothly as possible; then calculate the results you can expect when there are delays or other complications. If the difference between the two calculations is significant, there may be more risks associated with the implementation than originally believed.

Identifying Real-World Roadblocks

Performing a risk analysis is also important when analyzing a proposed new work concept because it helps the redesign team to identify possible impediments to implementation and plan ways early on to minimize or overcome them. Gaining a better knowledge of the problems they are likely to encounter may lead team members to make adjustments to the process design, incorporate increased training, or request additional resources.

Overlooking real or possible risks can mean major setbacks for any new process design, as the Airline Ticketing Corp. learned several years ago. When this company tried to reengineer the reservation system for airline travelers by developing electronic ticket machines, its early attempts were largely failures. The reason: Ticket machines were first installed behind the front desks of major hotels, and hotel clerks were reluctant to drop their work to operate the machines for guests. Now the company has invested several million dollars more in a self-service machine, to be located in shopping malls and supermarkets, that customers can operate themselves.[3]

To perform a detailed risk analysis, the redesign team should consider these six implementation issues and discuss how to deal with the roadblocks that may be encountered as a result of each one (Figure 7.6).

Resistance to change. You cannot expect to implement radical change without confronting some kind of opposition or resistance, and it could come

> • *Resistance to Change*
>   Will the change provoke resistance from employees, managers, or customers?
>
> • *Logistical Difficulties*
>   Will people have to be relocated or service disrupted?
>
> • *Resource Limitations*
>   Do we have the time, money, and human resources to implement the new design?
>
> • *Technological Obstacles*
>   Is the technology we need available, and do we have the right people to manage it?
>
> • *Control Issues*
>   Will the new roles created cause friction or discomfort?
>
> • *Training Drawbacks*
>   What will it take to provide training for the new skills required?

FIGURE 7.6.   Step 2: Identify Real-World Roadblocks

from any direction. Some managers may find it difficult to adjust to a team-based environment; for instance, customers may be reluctant to give up established sales or service relationships, or workers may be troubled by the thought of assuming additional responsibilities.

In one organization that reengineered, for example, the greatest threat to the success of its change effort came from its first-line supervisors. They perceived a move to increased participation as a personal loss of power and authority, and they refused to embrace the new organizational values. To win these people over, the company had to conduct a series of workshops designed specifically for them that outlined their contribution in a team-based environment and modeled the new roles they would be expected to play.

To anticipate any resistance to the changes they plan to implement, the redesign team should ask the following:

- Will the change create resistance from some employees, departments, or units?

- Will the change create resistance from some managers or supervisors?

- Will the change create resistance from some customers?

- What actions can we take to neutralize or minimize any potential resistance to the new design?

Logistical difficulties. The psychological aspects of change must be taken into account whenever you redesign jobs, alter reporting relationships, or introduce new technologies. But it's important to remember that there are also *physical* aspects to reengineering—moving people into new facilities, for example, rearranging office layouts, or bringing in new equipment—and these may create serious problems, too.

In one large Midwest organization, the reengineering plan involved such a major restructuring that just about every employee had to relocate to a different building or floor. To make the change as quickly and efficiently as possible, the company decided to move everyone in a single day. This had two beneficial results: It reinforced the message that the company was serious about change, and it kept to a minimum the interruptions in service that inevitably result whenever a company moves.

To anticipate any logistical difficulties their new design may entail, the redesign team should ask the following:

- Will people have to be relocated to make the new design work?

- Will service be disrupted during implementation of the new design?

- Will the transition to a new work design create a backlog of cases or paperwork?

- What actions can we take to ensure continued service during the changeover or to carry out the physical aspects of change as painlessly as possible?

Resource limitations. No matter how brilliant or imaginative the new design proposed, it's virtually worthless unless your organization has the human, financial, and technological resources to carry it through. What's more, even when the necessary resources exist, it cannot always be assumed that managers and other decision makers will agree to free them from the projects to which they are now allocated and rededicate them to the change effort.

One large service company that reengineered its payroll and accounting division, for example, found it difficult to make progress because some managers would not put aside the funds to cover the costs of change. Having learned its lesson, the company now requires those same managers to earmark at least 5 percent of their overall budget to so-called "program activities" to make sure that change and improvement remain top organizational priorities in the future.

To anticipate any problems that may result from limited resources, the redesign team should ask the following:

- How much money will be needed to implement the new design?

- Do we have the right people to maintain the new work process, or will we have to hire new employees or conduct additional training?

- Can we implement the new design in the space and with the equipment we already have?

- What actions can we take to keep additional investments of time, money, and human resources to a minimum?

Technological obstacles. Many organizations achieve significant breakthroughs in productivity or service quality by introducing advanced technologies or customized software applications. But reengineering strategies that rely too heavily on technology as a facilitator of change can sometimes backfire. When people are not prepared to accept new technologies or use them ineffectively, or when installation costs escalate, many of the gains that are expected can suddenly dissipate and new problems are created.

This happened at one large financial services company several years ago, where most of the technological innovations it was counting on either proved unworkable or failed to produce benefits until much later than had been planned. Just as bad, some of the new systems the company thought would bring about quantum leaps in efficiency ended up complicating the jobs of employees and making their work even more demanding than before.

To anticipate any technological obstacles that may result from the proposed new concept, the redesign team should ask the following:

- Is the technology we need available, and is it compatible with our existing systems?

- Do we have the expertise required to manage new or more sophisticated technologies?

- Are the information systems we have in place adequate to implement the proposed design or will new ones have to be developed?

- How can we minimize or eliminate the problems that new technologies might create?

Control issues. Major cultural changes are often an integral part of reengineering, and they may involve significant transfers of power and decision-making authority. But managers sometimes are not willing or prepared to give up their control—in solving production problems, setting work schedules, or making hiring decisions, for example—and lower-level workers may balk at the prospect of taking on additional work and new responsibilities.

Empowerment and participation are particularly difficult to implement in industries with long histories of hierarchical structures. One established insurance company, for example, strongly embraced these concepts early in its reengineering process, but its efforts to implement them caused widespread confusion and anxiety. Later the company realized that it should have provided clearer definitions for these terms and more training and support to guide workers and managers in their new roles.

To anticipate any delays or setbacks that may be caused by control issues, the redesign team should ask the following:

- Will some managers have to relinquish supervisory control or learn new behaviors?

- Do people at all levels feel comfortable in taking on new roles and responsibilities?

- Will the proposed changes create friction with unions or other labor organizations?

- What can we do to minimize or overcome the impediments to building a new and more participative work culture?

Training drawbacks. Organizations often underestimate the amount of time and energy they must invest to prepare people to function effectively in a reengineered environment. Whenever work teams are set up, for example, extensive and ongoing cross-training is usually needed to increase technical skills and knowledge, and keeping teams operating smoothly often requires additional training in problem solving, conflict resolution, and planning.

In making the transition to workstation professionals, one bank that reengineered had to reroute service calls for weeks at a time to accommodate training schedules for front-line workers. Because they had to learn all the functions that were once carried out by several back-office departments, these workers were frequently away from their desks and did not complete their training for well over a year.

To anticipate the challenges created by conducting extensive and ongoing training, the redesign team should ask the following:

- How long will it take people to learn the skills they need for the new design to work effectively?

- How many people will have to be trained?

- Are there training programs available that can provide the new skills needed or will customized programs have to be developed?

- What can we do to minimize the cost of training and the disruptions it may entail?

Identifying Potential Quick Hits

Though reengineering changes are often implemented over an extended period of time, the best redesign changes strive for both short-term and long-term impact. Some significant signs of performance improvement, in fact, should be delivered in the first 6 to 12 months of implementation (Figure 7.7).

A substantial and positive short-term impact is important for three reasons: (1) It helps maintain enthusiasm for the change process over the long term; (2) it helps sustain the energy needed to capture future improvements; and (3) it helps fund the investment that's required to make the reengineering project succeed.

One company in health systems management, for example, recently introduced an interstate network with a consortium of insurance companies that will revolutionize the way medical claims are processed. Although it may take several years for the full advantages of the network to be realized, the installation of only part of it now allows doctors and hospitals to verify the insurance coverage of patients far more easily through desktop computers. Although limited in scope, these benefits have helped the company create significant buy-in to the idea of processing health information electronically, and its customers are eagerly awaiting the day when the system will also provide deductible and co-payment information and file claims automatically.

In much the same way, members of the redesign team can make their proposed changes more attractive to others in their organization and help sell their recommendations by showing that the new design will have an immediate and positive impact. One way they can do that is by identifying potential "quick-hit" changes—that is, recommendations for change to the work process that can be implemented relatively easily and quickly and that will produce noticeable results right away.

- It helps maintain enthusiasm for the change process.

- It helps sustain the energy needed for future improvements.

- It helps fund the reengineering effort.

FIGURE 7.7.   Benefits of a Quick Hit

Potential quick-hit changes can often be located in these six areas (Figure 7.8):

1. *Areas where customer dissatisfaction is especially high.* If customers are complaining about delays in turnaround time, for example, is it possible to speed up the process simply by eliminating multiple approvals or bypassing individuals who do not add real value to the process? Or can you raise service levels quickly by developing a set of protocols for handling common customer inquiries or problems?

2. *Areas where recommended changes would not require relocation or extensive training.* Can you improve the quality of the product you sell merely by purchasing better raw materials, for example, or by raising the quality standards you set for suppliers? Can you cut costs fast by automating labor-intensive activities, by eliminating routine reports, or by discontinuing the storage of data that are rarely used?

3. *Areas where employees and their managers are eager for change.* Can you set up customer-centered teams to support front-line service workers, provide quick relief during periods of peak work loads, or distribute tasks more equitably? Can you make it easier for salespeople to sell your product or service just by providing them with better marketing materials or by reducing the number of forms you require from the field?

- Areas where customer dissatisfaction is especially high.

- Areas where recommended changes would not require relocation or extensive training.

- Areas where employees and their managers are eager for change.

- Areas where recommended changes can be made with existing technologies and information systems.

- Areas where the need for change is urgent and improvements must be made immediately.

- Areas where work steps or approvals can be eliminated easily.

FIGURE 7.8. Step 3: Identify Potential Quick Hits

4. *Areas where recommended changes can be made with existing technologies and information systems.* Can you easily eliminate bureaucratic bottlenecks by balancing work loads, by moving people closer together, or by redesigning required forms? Can you improve performance just by upgrading or repairing the equipment you now use or by making better use of it?

5. *Areas where the need for change is urgent and improvements must be made immediately.* Can you eliminate several steps in the work process or automate certain parts in order to improve response time quickly, fill orders faster, or eliminate a backlog of orders? Can you refine or improve operations at critical points in the service cycle to boost customer confidence and regain market share?

6. *Areas where work steps or approvals can be eliminated easily.* Can you achieve quick efficiencies by doing away with unnecessary checks and balances, by waiving the requirement for multiple copies, or by eliminating follow-up correspondence? Can you streamline the process right away by combining similar activities that are performed at different points in the process?

Preparing to Sell the Change Recommendation

Any team that's followed the redesign process we have outlined so far will have invested a great deal of time and energy into diagnosing the existing organization, generating new process concepts, and selecting the design option that appears to be the most promising. It will have carefully calculated the benefits and costs of the new design, identified the possible risks involved and found ways to minimize or overcome them, and then pinpointed changes that can be made quickly and easily. Finally, the time will come for the team to carry out its final responsibility: to present its ideas to the steering team and gain approval for implementation.

This is no small task. Making any presentation to senior management—especially one that coordinates public speaking with overheads or slides and accompanying written materials—can be a nerve-racking experience. And other factors may contribute significantly to compound that anxiety. Among the most troublesome is the possibility that the team may encounter some opposition to its change recommendations, disagreement with its analyses and evaluations, or skepticism that its new design will achieve the desired results.

For this reason, the redesign team will want to make sure its proposal is clear and convincing and that the presentation goes as smoothly as possible.

The best way to do that is for team members to prepare well for possible objections and criticisms and work diligently to effectively sell their recommendations (Figure 7.9). Here are three helpful suggestions:

Demonstrate significant contrasts. One way for the redesign team to promote the benefits of the changes it wants to make is to show exactly how the process design it's proposing is different from the existing one and what makes it better. A simple table (Figure 7.10) will allow the team to demonstrate these contrasts. (The column on the left lists a few of the criteria the team may want to use to highlight possible areas of significant difference.)

Develop effective presentation materials. Good presentation materials—a well-organized written proposal, for example, compelling charts and graphs, or visually attractive overheads or slides—should be considered an essential component of the redesign team's "sales strategy." *How* team members present their change recommendations can be just as important as *what* they want to say, so they should pay special attention to the materials they use to get their ideas across.

When developing their presentation materials, the members of the redesign team should follow these common preparation guidelines (Figure 7.11):

Consider visual appeal. There's no point in spending a lot of time researching and writing if the final proposal does not *look* even vaguely inviting. To make sure that others will actually read the proposal or examine the charts and graphs, remember that window dressing counts. Try to make the presentation materials as interesting and as attractive as possible.

Use the right headings. Think of headings as signposts and use them to telegraph the most important findings or conclusions. Avoid dull and generic

---

- Demonstrate significant contrasts.

- Develop effective presentation materials.

- Anticipate decision-maker questions.

FIGURE 7.9.   Step 4: Prepare to Sell the Change
Recommendation

Areas of Significant Difference	Existing Process	Proposed Design
Cycle time		
Customer service		
Quality		
Reliability		
Defect rate		
Operating costs		
Labor requirements		

FIGURE 7.10. A Simple Table for Demonstrating Contrasts

headings—like "Background" or "Analysis" or "Costs"—and try to come up with headings that grab people and tell them what to expect. Example: "New Design Cuts Costs and Defect Rates in Half."

Don't get fancy. When the design of presentation materials becomes too fancy or elaborate (through the use of unusual or ornate typefaces, for example), it creates a distraction from the essential points being made. So avoid visual clutter, and keep things simple and clean looking.

Don't skimp on white space. No one wants to reads acres of unbroken text or look at a cramped and crowded chart. So when preparing presentation

- Consider visual appeal.

- Use the right headings.

- Don't get fancy.

- Don't skimp on white space.

- Avoid data overload.

FIGURE 7.11. Presentation Materials Checklist

materials, always make sure there's plenty of white space to give the reader's eyes a rest. (*Tip:* In written materials, insert a blank line between paragraphs and use wide margins.)

Avoid data overload.

Don't think that the proposal will have a better chance of approval if people are inundated with production figures or financial estimates. An excessive reliance on numbers can actually make a presentation dull and difficult to understand, so include them only when they prove a point or provide clarification. Whenever possible, present them in a visual format: a chart, table, or graph, for example.[4]

Anticipate decision-maker questions.

At least part of the time devoted to planning the formal presentation should be spent preparing responses to questions the redesign team *expects* people to ask. No matter how clearly ideas are presented or how detailed the change recommendations, team members can be sure that those whose responsibility it is to approve what they are suggesting will feel obligated to give the proposal a thorough review.

What questions are they most likely to ask? Chances are good that many will focus on implementation costs, the redeployment of hiring of employees, and the logistical challenges of getting "from here to there." Here are some questions for which the team might want to consider preparing answers *in advance:*

- Is there any way that implementation costs can be reduced?

- Can the same proposal be implemented without additional hiring or training?

- How will you minimize service disruptions or production delays during the implementation period?

- What strategy will you use to "cut over" to the new process design?

- What structural or process changes will have to be made in other parts of the organization to accommodate the new design?

In preparing answers to these questions, the team may want to appoint "experts" among its members to specialize in different aspects of the new process or its implementation. (One person could be designated the authority on human and financial resource requirements, for example, and another could focus on new technologies or organizational structures.) This will ensure that the team has a firm grasp on all the major issues involved and allows its members to share more equitably the responsibility of responding to questions or criticisms.

Notes

1.   See "Banks Court Disenchanted Customers," *Wall Street Journal*, August 30, 1993, p. 35.

2.   See "More Service Stations Install New Machines for Paying at Pumps," *Wall Street Journal*, August 3, 1993.

3.   See "Ticketing Maverick Making Her Mark," *USA Today*, August 31, 1993, p. 83.

4.   These and other tips on preparing written presentation documents are included in Mary Holcombe and Judy Stein, *Writing for Decision Makers* (New York: Van Nostrand Reinhold, Inc., 1987).

8

The Final Phases: Implementing the New Design and Evaluating Results

There are three possible ways the steering team can respond to the reengineering recommendations (Figure 8.1). It can fully approve the recommendations for implementation; it can adopt the recommendations with modifications; or it can refuse to implement the recommendations and ask the redesign team to begin its work all over again.

Outright rejection rarely occurs, however. For even though the redesign team must formally seek approval for implementation, in most cases the design it recommends has been substantially *pre*sold and *pre*approved. That's because the steering team usually follows the work of the redesign team closely as it progresses through the idea-generating and concept-analysis phases, and it frequently provides input along the way. By the time the formal presentation takes place, many members of the steering team have become intimately familiar with the ideas being proposed, and there's relatively little for them to consider that's new.

That's not to say that steering teams blindly endorse the proposals made during these presentations or that redesign teams consistently get the green light to implement all their ideas. There have been several reengineering cases, in fact, where members of the steering team felt they needed additional time to discuss the ideas being proposed or decided to make considerable revisions to the recommended design.

In situations like these, any changes that are made are often based on business information to which only the steering team has access or on sudden shifts

1. Approve for implementation.

2. Adopt with modifications
   • changes in technology
   • changes in timing.

3. Reject implementation.

FIGURE 8.1.   Three Steering Team Responses to
Reengineering Recommendations

in the organization's strategic plan (due to an unexpected merger, perhaps, or a sudden downturn in revenues or profits). Whatever the reason, the changes the steering team calls for usually fall into one or both of the following categories:

Changes in technology. It's not uncommon for redesign teams to recommend an advanced new technology or computer system as part of its process redesign. But no matter how conscientious the team has been to establish the strategic fit of the proposed technology or determine its compatibility with existing systems, the financial investment it entails often makes steering teams pause and reconsider.

In one large organization that reengineered, for example, the redesign team recommended as part of its proposal an expensive new tracking system for a service operation. Although the steering team was convinced of the potential benefits of the system, it had serious doubts about whether the company could realistically afford it. In the end, the steering team announced that it would examine the proposal once again provided two conditions were met: that an extensive search of possible vendors was conducted and that the redesign team presented an accurate tally of all the costs involved.

Changes in timing. Steering teams are also inclined to revise the tentative timetables included in many redesign proposals. They may decide to speed up the implementation process, for example, because they feel that competitive pressures are growing and results are needed right away. Or they may suggest slowing down the process to ensure that training in new skills takes hold or that the costs of implementation are spread out over time.

In one company that reengineered, the redesign team presented a proposal to be implemented in four stages, but without providing much of an explanation, the steering team would approve only the first stage and the last. Although it felt rebuffed, the redesign team agreed to modify its schedule and to cut the implementation period by more than half. Eventually, it was revealed that the business units involved in the two stages eliminated from the proposal were to be dissolved, and that was information the steering team was unwilling to share at the time the proposal was presented.

Decommissioning the Redesign Team

Even when all the members of the steering team approve the new process design without reservations, they should not simply rubber stamp the proposal on the day that it's presented. A better response is for the steering team to listen to the proposal attentively, collect copies to take home and annotate, and request a few days to review the recommendations thoroughly.

What's the point of dragging out the process? By taking the time to carefully deliberate the proposed changes, the steering team sends a strong message that it views these changes as vitally important to the organization and that it respects the work of the redesign team enough to give them serious consideration.

Some ceremony to formally decommission the redesign team and celebrate its achievements should be held at this point in the reengineering process. By honoring the members of the redesign team and publicly acknowledging what they've accomplished, the steering team serves two purposes (Figure 8.2): (1) It educates people in the progress that's been made toward reaching the organization's reengineering goals—which is important to maintaining morale and momentum; and (2) it inaugurates the fourth phase of reengineering: implementation.

To make sure people thoroughly understand what lies ahead, the steering team may also choose to relay information through other communication

---

- To educate people in the progress that's been made.

- To inaugurate the implementation phase.

FIGURE 8.2. Reasons for Honoring the Redesign Team

channels—the company newsletter, for example, town meetings, or an internal letter from the president. Because expectations are bound to run high at this time, an effort should be made to inform people, at the very least, about which recommendations suggested by the redesign team have been accepted and what will be the process involved in completing their implementation.

In this chapter, you will learn the two steps involved in carrying out the implementation phase of the reengineering process:

1. Developing an implementation plan.

2. Resolving tactical implementation issues.

Finally, you will learn what's involved in monitoring and measuring your implementation results.

Developing an Implementation Plan

Once the recommendations of the redesign team have been finalized and approved, the next step in the reengineering process is to translate them into reality (Figure 8.3). Another cross-functional team, the implementation planning group, is usually charged with making this happen. Though the redesign team may stay on in some organizations to execute implementation, it's a good idea to assemble a new group for this function for two reasons: (1) It injects new energy at a critical point in the reengineering process, and (2) it allows you to recruit people who excel in different areas—like planning and project management—and who may succeed better at implementation.

The makeup of the implementation planning group often depends on which areas of the organization will be affected by the recommendations proposed. But because of the training and technological implications of most reengineering changes, this group almost always includes specialists in human resources

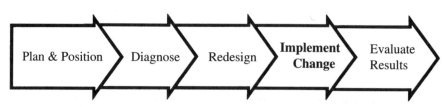

FIGURE 8.3.   The Five Phases of Reengineering

and information management. Although some members of the redesign team may qualify for membership in the group, they should not be included unless they have strong planning skills or a background in project management.

The ultimate goal of the implementation planning group is to develop a detailed checklist of the activities that must be carried out to implement the reengineering changes and to establish specific target dates and accountabilities. But before the group can reach the point of handing out assignments, it must come up with a good implementation plan: a clear road map for taking the organization from where it is now to where it wants to go (Figure 8.4).

Perform a gap analysis. A thorough "gap analysis" is the first step in developing a reengineering implementation plan. Its purpose is to help the implementation planning group identify and assess all the areas that will be affected by reengineering and to decide what actions must be taken within those areas to bring about the desired changes.

One way for the group to conduct a gap analysis is to ask itself a series of broad questions to establish the overall scope of implementation, and then to focus within specific areas to flesh out the details of the changes to be made. For example, the implementation planning group might begin by asking the following:

- What are the *job design* implications of the proposed new design?

- How will our *organizational structure* have to be modified to adopt this design?

- What will be the impact on our *technology and information systems?*

- What are the implications for our *compensation, recognition, and reward systems?*

- Do changes have to be made in our *facilities and physical layout* to implement the recommended design?

- What are the *training* implications of the proposed changes?

- Perform a gap analysis.

- Integrate tasks and subtasks.

FIGURE 8.4.   Step 1: Develop an Implementation Plan

Within each broad area of expected change, the group then asks more specific questions to determine what tasks need to be carried out to implement the new design. In the area of training, for example, the group might ask: What are the technical training needs of the new customer teams that will be formed? Will different service skills be required? What interpersonal skills must team members learn in order to work together effectively? What skills must managers master to carry out their new roles as team leaders and coaches?

Although the implementation planning process should be carried out as quickly as possible—to maintain momentum, a final implementation plan should be submitted to the steering team within 2 or 3 weeks—it's also important for the group to investigate every aspect of needed change carefully and not to overlook any important details. The more thorough the gap analysis, the more comprehensive the implementation plan will be and the more likely it will succeed at achieving the intended results.

Integrate tasks and subtasks. The next step in developing an implementation plan is to combine all the tasks identified through the gap analysis into a coordinated sequence of required activities, with specific time schedules, target dates for completion, and assigned accountabilities. Many organizations that reengineer now rely on sophisticated project-management software to help them set up their final implementation plan, although in most cases all that's really necessary is a pencil and paper, a calendar, and good planning skills.

The steering team may provide little or no input while the gap analysis is being performed, but it should review and approve the final implementation plan to make sure that it's clear and workable, that the timing makes sense, and that it's likely to achieve the desired results. How will the steering team know whether the implementation plan is a "good" plan? Although professional planners are constantly changing their minds about what is an effective plan and what isn't, there are several characteristics that most agree are essential to a good implementation plan (Figure 8.5):

1. *It lays out activities in sequence.* Putting the activities that must be carried out into the proper order is the very heart of planning. Without a definite sequence, some activities may be executed prematurely, and others may occur too late. That's why it always improves the implementation process when planners decide (a) what steps must be finished before others can begin and (b) what steps can occur simultaneously.

Setting up sequences of activities usually involves a lot of trial and error. But flowcharts—which depict when each step takes place and how it relates to

---

- *It lays out activities in sequence.*

- *It includes target dates and follow-up dates.*

- *It defines who's responsible for each activity.*

- *It contains a review mechanism.*

- *It allows for contingencies.*

- *It's easily understood by the people who will implement it.*

FIGURE 8.5. An Effective Implementation Plan

the others—can help. They provide a visual guide people can follow as the implementation process unfolds, and the act of preparing them gives planners the chance to experiment with various sequences *before* the activities are actually carried out.

2. *It includes target dates and follow-up dates.* Plans are tools for making the best use of people's time, so they must include exact references to time. These include "target dates," which establish when an event will take place or when a result is expected, and "follow-up dates," which track progress toward a particular target.

A good plan will also schedule times when the steering team or the implementation planning group can reconvene to consider whether particular results are being achieved or what can be done to improve results.

3. *It defines who's responsible for each activity.* Lack of supervision during the implementation phase is a common cause of failure in reengineering projects. Changes are announced with great fanfare and everyone scurries around for a while, but when the dust settles, not much has really happened, and employees may be even less productive than before. New process designs may look great on paper, but when no one is standing by to spot and fix the day-to-day problems that may pop up, the probability of failure is significantly increased.

Designating people by name to direct and control each activity within the plan is the only way to prevent this from happening. For the most part, supervisors or team leaders should be assigned these responsibilities, although lower-level employees should be encouraged to carry them out.

4. *It contains a review mechanism.* When we plan, we always do it on the basis of a certain set of assumptions (an expected volume of sales, for example, or the belief that market conditions will remain stable). But over time, some of our assumptions may prove to be wrong. That's why plans should be reviewed regularly, and a review mechanism (stipulating when the review should take place and who should do it) should be built right in to the plan.

This isn't to say that implementation plans should constantly be modified, however. Part of the art of management, after all, is knowing when to stand firm on a plan—despite the winds of change—and when to adjust the plan to reflect reality.

5. *It allows for contingencies.* The wise planner thinks ahead: about how business conditions may change (which may require adjustments to the implementation plan) or what may go wrong when scheduled activities are carried out (which may require additional measures or corrective action).

Once you begin to think about these uncertainties, you realize just how many there may be. But the purpose of contingency planning is not to prepare yourself for every remote possibility. Rather, it's to find what events are more likely to happen than others—or where foul-ups may occur—and then to outline alternative courses of action.

Although contingency planning takes time, it may actually save you time and effort in the long run. Why? Because if you have done a good job of contingency planning, you can react more quickly and effectively whenever a crisis strikes. Those who fail to plan for contingencies spend precious time debating and deliberating when they're in a situation that calls for quick action.

6. *It's easily understood by those who will implement it.* Plans written in archaic, esoteric, or highly technical language usually are not effective. People will perform well only when they know what it is they have to do. And because they are the ones who will implement the plan or be affected by it, it's only right that they should easily understand what it says and means.

Resolving Tactical Implementation Issues

The implementation phase can be the most exciting part of the reengineering process, because that's when you finally begin to see the results of your change efforts. But it can also be the riskiest, and there are two reasons why. First, it takes the longest time to carry out—up to 12 months in most large organizations—and that multiplies the possibilities for errors and mistakes.

Second, it deals with *real* change—not change on a conceptual level—and that's a far more difficult and challenging goal to achieve.

A good implementation plan helps guide organizations as they carry out their reengineering changes, but there are bound to be tactical and logistical issues that will surface along the way. Fortunately, enough organizations have already reengineered that we now know what these issues typically are and what the appropriate responses should be. What follows is a series of guidelines that address some of the more problematic implementation issues that reengineering organizations are likely to confront (Figure 8.6).

Maintain a realistic perspective on participation. The planning, diagnostic, and redesign phases of reengineering are driven by relatively small groups of people: the senior executive committee, the steering team, the diagnostic team, or the redesign team. But the implementation phase provides an opportunity for much wider participation, which is both necessary and desirable. Tapping into the skills and experience of people at all levels in the organization can help ensure that the reengineering changes you want carried out are made quickly and that all the day-to-day details that are part of getting the work done are incorporated in the transformation.

In their enthusiasm for greater involvement, however, some organizations fall into the trap of promoting participation for its own sake, and that may actually have an adverse impact on implementation. Ironically, one potential

---

- Maintain a realistic perspective on participation.

- Make change happen quickly.

- Communicate with internal and external customers.

- Anticipate higher levels of stress.

- Create a talent bank for displaced workers.

FIGURE 8.6. Step 2: Resolve Tactical Implementation Issues

problem is that it can slow down the process. When teams of people are charged with executing changes that individuals can handle more efficiently, decisions tend to be made committee-style—with action taking a back seat to deliberation—and the pace of change can slow down considerably.

Another pitfall in the drive to achieve universal participation is that people who lack the right skills are also included in the implementation process, or there's sometimes a mismatch between what people are good at and what they are asked to do. When managers are charged with redesigning work flows, for example, or clerks are assigned to making structural reforms, there's little chance that an organization will accomplish implementation with optimal results.

To avoid these problems, build a strong network of implementation teams throughout your organization, but deploy them only when the combined skills of the people involved will guarantee that the changes that need to be made will be implemented quickly and effectively. By maintaining a realistic perspective on the benefits of participation, you can take full advantage of the talent that lies within your organization but sidestep the problems that result when involvement isn't appropriate.

Make change happen quickly. The pace of change is often a critical issue during the implementation phase. Admittedly, it takes time to change the way an organization operates, and the more fundamental or far-reaching the change recommendations to be carried out, the longer it may take to see results that matter. But when change occurs too slowly, energy levels dip, people become diverted by other considerations, and the reengineering process can lose momentum.

Those who work in the trenches have especially high expectations that, once implementation starts, change will happen quickly. And when it doesn't, they often become disappointed or disillusioned. If 3 or 4 months pass, and there's no discernable difference in what people are doing or how the organization functions, then reengineering may be judged to be just another improvement "exercise" or, worse, a sign that management is unwilling or unable to deal with meaningful change.

Some organizations aggravate this problem by insisting on conducting additional diagnostic work before implementation begins or by continuing to tinker with the recommended changes to iron out potential design problems. But in their desire to achieve perfection, they may end up stalling the implementation process and reinforcing doubts about the effectiveness of

reengineering or the organization's commitment to see real change carried through.

For these reasons, organizations that reengineer should introduce some kind of visible change at the very start of the implementation process. Even though people may not be able to *measure* the results of implementation for 4 or 5 months (in terms of increased revenues, for example, or higher levels of service quality), some indicators of change can be integrated into the process right from the start. Training in new technical or team skills, for instance, can be initiated as soon as implementation begins, and this gives people the feeling that something different is happening, that energies are being directed toward new goals, and that real change is imminent.

It's also wise to accelerate implementation whenever possible. Although there's sometimes a tendency to slow the process down to make sure that changes are implemented correctly, it's better to get through the pain of transition quickly rather than to prolong it, even if it means sacrificing precision in execution. What's more, perfection may actually be a counterproductive goal when reengineering; by the time it takes you to achieve it, new business conditions may exist that could render your reengineering choices invalid.

Communicate with internal and external customers. Another important issue during implementation is deciding whether or not to tell customers about the reengineering changes you are making and, if you do decide to tell, exactly how much to disclose. We believe the approach you take should vary, depending on the type of customer you are dealing with.

External customers should be told only as much as is necessary to explain changes in service or to satisfy queries about internal operations. And the information they receive should come from those who deal with your customers most: your salespeople, for example, or your front-line service providers. If you feel strongly that you will benefit from publicizing your reengineering effort, stick to general messages like, "We're changing to serve you better" or "We're reengineering with our customers in mind." It's usually *not* a good idea to make commitments based on what you hope to achieve or to share specific reengineering goals. Why? It may establish expectations among customers that you may not be able to meet.

Internal customers, however, should be kept fully informed of the reengineering effort, and whomever you select to communicate with them should be powerful or persuasive enough to win their approval and support. One department that reengineered in a large insurance company, for example, enlisted the marketing department in explaining reengineering to its agents in the field. Because their jobs would be directly affected by the changes being made, the department felt it needed professional help to win their cooperation and sell the benefits of the project internally.

Anticipate higher levels of stress. One financial services organization says it recorded a 15 percent jump in productivity during its implementation phase. This is highly unusual. In most cases, organizations barely manage to keep their head above water during implementation, because this is a period of increased stress and confusion when productivity is likely to suffer.

It's unrealistic to expect operations to continue seamlessly when there's so much change and activity taking place. But it is possible to anticipate higher levels of stress and to devise effective strategies for coping with them and moderating their impact. Especially important is the need to shield customers from the internal chaos that may be caused by implementation and to make sure that there are no major interruptions in service.

How is it possible to set up new work teams or conduct extensive training, for example, yet still man the phone lines, maintain production schedules, or prevent a backlog of orders? One piece of good advice is to avoid implementing critical changes during periods of peak volume. If your sales revenues, service cycles, or production targets fluctuate throughout the year, remember that it's always easier to endure the rigors of implementation when there are fewer demands on people's time and attention. Another implementation tip: Consider alternative work and training schedules. Hire part-time help or encourage employees to put in overtime, for example, or conduct training sessions after work hours or on weekends.

Plans also should be developed for how to handle customers when changes are being made in service delivery. If you are switching from a functional setup to one-stop service teams, for example, then uniform practices should be established for directing customers to their new contacts in the organization or for communicating how the new system will work, when it will go into effect, and what changes can be expected. If a temporary falloff in service quality is unavoidable, then customers should at least be informed of the reasons why.

Create a talent bank for displaced workers. Another way for companies to fill in the service or production gaps that may occur during implementation is to make good use of the people who are displaced through reengineering. In the past, those whose jobs were eliminated or significantly reshaped because of new technologies, job redesigns, or structural changes were often let go. But in recent years, a different approach has proved to be more productive. At companies like AAL and The Principal Financial Group, "talent banks" were set up so workers could be retrained for new jobs, counseled for outplacement to other parts of the organization or to other companies, or assigned to temporary positions during the implementation stage.

Organizations that strive to achieve an immediate payback from reengineering through layoffs often pay a hefty price down the road. When employees see their co-workers forced out the door, they are less likely to support the changes that reengineering entails, may demonstrate evidence of increased stress and reduced morale, or even engage in activities to sabotage the success of reengineering. So unless a company is in severe financial straits—and has no option but to cut labor costs—we strongly urge its leaders to set up some kind of talent bank during the implementation phase.

There are three benefits to be gained from the talent bank approach (Figure 8.7):

1. *It diminishes the emotional impact of downsizing.* A talent bank sends the important message that displaced workers are valuable assets to be utilized, not extraneous workers to be discarded. Although some of the people who lose their jobs through reengineering may decide to leave the company, a talent bank assures those who choose to stay that they can still make a valid contribution to the organization and continue to work with dignity and respect.

2. *It provides alternative career opportunities.* A talent bank offers outplacement services for displaced workers or helps them locate jobs in other departments or units within the same organization. Because there are always some

---

- To diminish the emotional impact of downsizing.

- To provide alternative career opportunities.

- To align existing talents with future skill requirements.

FIGURE 8.7. Reasons for Creating a Talent Bank

people who refuse to adjust to a reengineered work environment or never master the new skills required, a talent bank can establish alternative career opportunities for them by providing emotional, clerical, and professional support while they look for employment elsewhere.

3. *It aligns existing talents with future skill requirements.* In most cases, all the talent that an organization needs to succeed at reengineering can be found in its existing labor pool, though extensive training in new technical or interpersonal skills may be required. Yet what we find during most implementations is that the bulk of this training takes place at lower levels of the organization, and new skill requirements for managers are largely ignored. A talent bank can help fill this training gap and provide remaining managers with the skills they need to function successfully in the future.

Surprisingly, many companies that are unwilling to tolerate skill deficiencies in clerical or technical workers will allow their managers to stay on without requiring them to change. But when an organization shifts from the traditional command-and-control style of management and adopts the principles of empowerment in the course of reengineering, its managers must accept new responsibilities as team leaders and coaches and learn how to operate differently. A talent bank can provide training for managers in these areas and reinforce the new skills required in a team-based environment.

Monitoring and Measuring
Implementation Results

There are three sets of measurements you should develop to help you gauge your progress as you proceed through the implementation phase (Figures 8.8 and 8.9). The first will determine how well you are doing in carrying out the changes recommended by the redesign team. The second will determine how well your business is doing as you make the recommended changes. And the

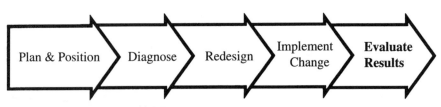

FIGURE 8.8. The Five Phases of Reengineering

1. Transition measurements.

2. Control measurements.

3. Outcome measurements.

FIGURE 8.9.   Three Sets of Reengineering
Measurements

third will determine how well those changes are helping you achieve your reengineering goals.

Transition measurements. As you work through the implementation phase of reengineering, one way to track your success is to compare what you have accomplished, at regular intervals, to the objectives outlined in the implementation plan. Ask yourself, for example: Are you carrying out the changes as outlined in the implementation plan? Are you meeting the interim deadlines and target dates established for completion? Are there enough implementation teams to ensure that the recommended changes are being made smoothly and efficiently?

To find out whether you are falling behind schedule and how much you may need to accelerate the process to get back on track, develop a flow chart of events as you go along and compare it to your implementation timetable. Do not be surprised if you find that there are discrepancies between the two, however. It's never possible to implement reengineering changes exactly as planned, although you should strive to achieve at least 80 percent of what you hoped to accomplish and develop a strategy for carrying out the rest of the plan at a later time.

Control measurements. It's also important to monitor performance during implementation to make sure you are meeting your short-term business objectives and that variations in production or service quality, for example, fall within an acceptable range. When organizations reengineer, they sometimes focus so intently on achieving their long-term improvement goals that they neglect the demands of day-to-day operations or *undermanage* their existing business.

This oversight can easily be remedied by establishing a series of quantitative measurements to track output and quality levels routinely throughout the implementation phase (Figure 8.10). In most organizations, some measurements like these already exist—calculating the number of orders filled per day or week, for example, tracking the responsiveness to customer requests or complaints, or computing daily production. And managers need only remind themselves to review these indicators regularly to make sure that the process of implementation does not cause the organization to fall outside acceptable limits of control.

Outcome measurements. The true test of the effectiveness of your implementation plan is whether the changes you are introducing are producing the results you want and are helping you achieve your reengineering goals. When you were generating new design concepts and selecting potential candidates, you relied on *predicted outcomes* to measure the value of each design. Now you can measure the value of the design you chose by comparing *actual outcomes* to the projections you made.

The purpose of developing and tracking outcome measurements is in what they tell you to do:

- When your results match or exceed your projections, your measurements indicate that you should proceed as planned.

- When your results fall short of your projections, your measurements indicate that you should make adjustments to improve results.

How do you know what needs to be measured? One good way to make that determination is to look back at the work of the redesign team in formulating new design concepts and evaluating candidate concepts. At that time,

---

- To determine if you're falling behind schedule.

- To maintain control over day-to-day operations.

- To decide what to pay attention to and improve.

FIGURE 8.10. Objectives of Quantitative Measurements

the team used the original reengineering success targets to compare designs, and it drew up a list of criteria to assess the benefits of each design (see Chapter 6). Those targets and criteria can now provide important clues as to what aspects of the process should be measured over time and where you should focus your efforts if improvement is needed.

To ensure that your measurements provide a comprehensive assessment of the new design, it also helps to reapply the C.E.O. thinking practiced back then to identify the performance criteria that are critical to each important stakeholder—your customers, your employees, and your organization—and develop appropriate measurement tools (Figure 8.11). For example, if responsiveness is a key customer concern, then the speed with which you process orders would be a valuable measurement tool. If increased profitability has been established as a reengineering goal for your organization, then you might want to measure costs per transaction or sales margins. If job variety and regular performance feedback are important to employees, then you might want to develop a survey to measure job satisfaction.

The matrix in Figure 8.12 will help you align the performance criteria that are critical to each stakeholder with the possible tools you can use to measure them.

In order to be useful, a measurement tool must be:

Necessary   It provides critical information on a key performance indicator.

Reliable   It produces consistent results no matter who uses it or when it's used.

Accurate   It's precise and tells you exactly what you want to know.

Practical   It can be used and understood easily.

FIGURE 8.11. Requirements of an Effective Measurement Tool

	Performance Criteria	Performance Measures
Customer		
Employee		
Organization		

FIGURE 8.12.   Stakeholder Matrix

Developing a measurement system is vital to your improvement effort because it tells you not only how well you are doing in relation to your reengineering targets, but also how well you are improving over time. Both kinds of information are necessary if reengineering is to help you initiate and maintain a process of continuous improvement.

It's important to remember that customer needs and expectations are always changing, and any process improvements you make now will some day have to be reexamined and thought through once again. By then, you and many of the others who participated in this reengineering project may have moved on. But you can be sure that the improvement process will continue if you set up an effective and ongoing measurement system now. It will provide a solid foundation for any future reengineering work and for any refinements and adjustments that will have to be made along the way.

9

Pitfalls and Pointers: Twelve Lessons for Reengineering Success

Even with clear targets and a broadly shared understanding of the need for change, reengineering efforts can head off course, flounder, and even fail. What can go wrong? Given the complexity of the process and the scope of the changes involved, there are any number of possibilities. An organization may become diverted by new market conditions and abandon the effort, for example. It may not be able to maintain the level of participation needed to ensure the acceptance of change. Or it may simply lose the energy and motivation it felt at the start and end up producing results that fall far short of what was expected.

Fortunately, these catastrophes typically do not occur; most organizations that reengineer, in fact, would describe their change effort as a success. And by closely following the process outlined in this book, they are able to achieve significant—if not dramatic—improvements in productivity and quality, and they enhance their competitive position markedly.

That's not to say that organizations that have reengineered did not experience problems, or that they would not do things differently if they had to repeat the process. What pitfalls did they encounter, and what pointers could they pass along to organizations that have yet to reengineer? We have compiled a list of 12 important lessons learned from companies' reengineering experiences. You may be able to apply some of these lessons to any process of large-scale organizational change, although all of them were relayed to us by managers who have reengineered and are described here specifically within that context.

Lesson 1: Overinvest in Preparation

Even when pressing business imperatives are what motivate an organization to change—and it needs to see results fast—experience demonstrates that thorough preparation is critical to the success of reengineering (Figure 9.1). Any time an organization undertakes wholesale change, the shoot-from-the-hip approach is inappropriate and will surely undermine efforts to achieve significant and lasting results.

What *is* adequate preparation? In some cases, organizations need to conduct an honest assessment of their financial and manpower resources before they can proceed, whereas others must first create the proper mind-set. When GE's Financial Services Organization reengineered, for example, its senior managers decided to first formulate a new vision statement to herald the coming change in business direction. Then they conducted a series of town meetings at all FSO locations to raise awareness of why the organization had to change and how they were going to do it.

Preparation is especially important when a company is *not* in a state of crisis and there's no apparent need for change. That was the case at AAL in 1985, before the company reengineered and officially launched its "Transformation" program. But there the CEO was able to prepare people for change—and stimulate feelings of dissatisfaction with the status quo—by conducting one-on-one interviews with his top people and asking them three simple questions: What are the company's strengths? What are its weaknesses? And if you had the chance to change anything you could, what would it be?

- Create the proper mind-set.

- Conduct an honest assessment of resources.

- Formulate a new vision statement.

FIGURE 9.1. Lesson 1: Overinvest in Preparation

Lesson 2: Don't Just Communicate; Tell the Truth!

Insufficient communication is a weakness organizations consistently demonstrate when they reengineer, and in hindsight, many realize that they should have done more in this area. One large insurance company, for example, made communication a top priority when it started to reengineer: newsletters were published, classes were held on special business topics, and town meetings were scheduled during lunch hours. But over time the company became sidetracked by other issues, its executives later admitted, and it became less diligent at maintaining its initial communication strategy.

Other organizations have voiced similar regrets, and some of them add this advice for those that are new to reengineering: Don't just communicate; tell the truth (Figure 9.2)! It's important to treat employees like adults—and work to sustain an open and honest dialogue with them—especially when they are being asked to participate more, assume greater responsibility, and make a bigger contribution.

Many organizations still exhibit the paternalistic behaviors that were common to companies in earlier days, and they tend to protect their people from unpleasant realities. But it's important to remember that, during a demanding and disruptive change effort like reengineering, employees will anticipate the worst anyway, so there's little to be gained from sugarcoating bad news or censoring information. Besides, when organizations commit themselves to sharing the truth, they gain trust and credibility in the eyes of their people, and those are critical qualities to have during periods of sacrifice and hard work.

- Treat employees like adults.

- Sustain an open and honest dialogue.

- Don't sugarcoat bad news.

FIGURE 9.2.   Lesson 2: Communicate the Truth

Lesson 3: Beware of Fits and Starts; Focus on Execution

Although it's only natural to want to slow down and take a break every once in a while, it's important to maintain a steady pace when reengineering. Moving in fits and starts can drag the process out and actually deplete organizational energies, as some companies have experienced (Figure 9.3). Why? Once you stop, it makes it all the more difficult to regain your momentum, and you may have to gear up all over again just to continue.

Some companies have problems with continuity because they stall or become mired in a particular reengineering phase. One organization, for example, allowed a significant amount of time to elapse between diagnosis and redesign because the steering team felt overwhelmed by the possibilities for change and could not make a final decision about what to reengineer.

Whenever an organization reaches an impasse like this, it should bring its reengineering leaders together and use whatever strategy-assessment, problem-solving, or priority-setting techniques are needed to jump start the process again. If necessary, outside help can be brought in to facilitate decision making and help the organization reach a level of understanding or agreement that will allow it to move on.

- Try to maintain a steady pace.

- If you reach an impasse, jump start the process with outside help, if necessary.

FIGURE 9.3. Lesson 3: Focus on Execution

Lesson 4: Expect the Best and Worst from People

Because reengineering involves extensive and fundamental change, it often requires that people expand their capabilities and do things they never did before. Frequently, they are asked to play new and more demanding roles during the process—business strategist, process analyst, or organizational architect, for example—and are expected to take on more challenging jobs when it's over. In most cases, people rise to the occasion, and they demonstrate talents that previously went untapped or unrecognized. But if reengineering can help bring out the best in people, as many organizations have reminded us, the stress and uncertainties it creates can also bring out their worst (Figure 9.4).

It's not unusual for people to experience some mental or emotional distress during reengineering, and that can have a negative impact on their behavior. They may refuse to cooperate with co-workers or become belligerent with supervisors, for example, or the quality of their work may simply deteriorate. That's why stress-reduction workshops are sometimes beneficial when companies reengineer, especially if jobs will be lost during the process or redesigned to include responsibilities that are significantly increased.

It also helps to educate people about change at the start of reengineering and to provide them with the skills they need to manage change better. When people develop a thorough understanding of what's likely to happen when an organization undertakes large-scale change, they are able to prepare themselves better psychologically for the process ahead of them and adapt more easily to new demands and expectations.

- Educate people about what's likely to happen.

- Provide skills that help people manage change.

- Conduct stress-reduction workshops.

FIGURE 9.4.   Lesson 4: Expect the Best and Worst from People

Lesson 5: Recognize Organizational Strengths and Build on Them

No matter how much we talk about reengineering in terms of "total," "radical," or "fundamental" change, few organizations are able to relinquish all the work processes, technological systems, and management practices they have taken years to develop and rebuild themselves from scratch. Nor, necessarily, should they. It's important to try to retain at least some elements of the existing organization whenever you reengineer, and there are two important reasons why.

First, every organization has certain strengths that it should work to build on, not abandon (Figure 9.5). It could be the loyal and dedicated work force you know you can count on to make the new organization succeed. Or it could be the popular, collegial approach you use to determine business strategy. Another example: When NationsBank reengineered its International Services Operation, some of the service teams that were created decided to organize themselves by region and others by product line. Although the service team concept was new to NationsBank, one aspect of the old organization did not change: a strong commitment to doing whatever it takes to satisfy local customer needs.

Another reason to carry over elements of the existing organization is that it adds stability to the change process. Remember, it can be frightening for people when every aspect of their work environment is radically redesigned or discarded, and they gain reassurance when something they are familiar with continues or remains the same.

- Don't abandon or discard organizational strengths.

- Retain elements of stability or familiarity.

FIGURE 9.5. Lesson 5: Recognize Organizational Strengths

Lesson 6: Keep the Process Line-Driven

Reengineering focuses primarily on the redesign of business processes, so line involvement is absolutely essential (Figure 9.6). That's because the people who actually perform or manage the jobs that add value for the customer are the ones who thoroughly understand the existing work processes and are best qualified to determine how they could be made better.

- Recruit line managers and those who perform jobs that add value for the customer.

- Limit the participation of staff people and outside consultants.

FIGURE 9.6.   Lesson 6: Keep the Process Line-Driven

Reengineering is far less effective when it's driven by staff people or, worse, consultants. Not only do these "outsiders" lack the experience and hands-on knowledge that are common to line workers, their recommendations for change are usually more difficult to sell internally, and that makes implementation all the more difficult.

That was the case in a large bank that wanted to redesign its service, sales, and product management business processes. As in other organizations that reengineer, a small redesign team was formed that eventually made a number of solid recommendations. But the fact that its core members consisted largely of administrators generated stiff resistance, and the team had to return to the drawing board again and again to come up with new ideas. In short, the lack of line participation was a drain on the team's credibility and undermined its overall effectiveness.

Lesson 7: Maintain Senior-Management Involvement

Although it seems an obvious point to make, the importance of senior-management involvement is one of the first issues we discuss with organizations that decide to reengineer (Figure 9.7). Unfortunately, what we say does not always sink in. Why not? Once they have blessed a reengineering effort, many senior managers lose interest in the process, and they tend to leave the work of implementation to others.

Although all too common, this kind of behavior can have a detrimental impact on reengineering results. One reason is that disinterest can be contagious, especially when it starts at the top. What's more, organizations have

- Include senior management in change implementation.

- Emphasize the message that senior management expects and encourages change.

- Maintain senior-management visibility through town meetings.

FIGURE 9.7.   Lesson 7: Maintain Senior-Management Involvement

implemented so many improvement efforts by now that many of their people demonstrate a wait-and-see attitude before becoming truly engaged. So when senior managers fail to become active participants in reengineering, it's unlikely that those lower down in the organizational ranks will commit themselves wholeheartedly to change.

Ongoing communication through newsletters, memos, and town meetings is one way senior management can maintain its visibility in the change process and express its support. But informal communication is just as important. Each and every day, senior managers must work to clear roadblocks for their people involved in reengineering and use reinforcement and recognition to maintain enthusiasm and focus. Above all, they must continually emphasize the message that change is encouraged and expected, and that they will provide whatever assistance they can to those who will work hard to implement it.

Lesson 8: Don't Impose Your Change Agenda on Customers

Its strong customer focus is one of the characteristics we often use to distinguish reengineering from other change strategies. But losing sight of the customer is, ironically, one of the biggest pitfalls of the process (Figure 9.8). How can this happen? When companies reengineer, executing their change agenda often becomes their number one priority. And to get the job done, they sometimes concentrate so strongly on internal matters that they shut themselves off from the outside world.

- Don't become sidetracked by internal matters.

- Remain sensitive to changing customer needs.

- Redirect change efforts in line with market shifts.

FIGURE 9.8. Lesson 8: Don't Impose Change Agenda on Customers

Although this may seem natural, it can be dangerous at a time like ours, when customer expectations and market conditions are changing rapidly. Just imagine, for example, if a health care company were to ignore what's happening in its marketplace during the 18 to 24 months it takes to reengineer. When the process is over, it may suddenly find itself playing in an entirely different ball game and emerge from the change effort ill equipped to compete. And these days, much the same could be said for companies in many other industries, including insurance, computer electronics, banking, retail, and transportation.

No matter how easy it is to become sidetracked by internal considerations, companies that reengineer must work diligently to remain sensitive to their customers' needs and expectations and, when necessary, redirect their change efforts in response to market shifts. Otherwise, they may end up reengineering backwards—imposing their agenda on their customers—and lose touch with the people most critical to their reengineering success.

Lesson 9: Use Technology to Enable— Not Drive—Organizational Change

Despite the popular impression that information technology is a driver of change when companies reengineer, many of the managers who have been through the process have told us just the opposite: System conversions are sometimes so complex or intractable that technology actually can lag behind other organizational changes, and for reengineering to proceed, it must often be conducted as a two-track process (Figure 9.9).

- Don't wait for new technologies to kick in before making changes.

- If necessary, implement reengineering as a two-track process.

FIGURE 9.9. Lesson 9: Use Technology to Enable Change

In one organization that reengineered, the installation of an integrated platform at all its locations was a primary objective when it began to reengineer. But 2 years later, the new system still was not up and running, and the company had to redirect its change efforts to keep from falling behind schedule. In another case, a large insurance company decided to reengineer *after* converting to a new system. But more than a year after jobs had been redesigned and the organization restructured, major technological problems were still being ironed out, and the company began to think seriously about shifting to yet another computer system.

Once implemented, new technologies can enable an organization to operate differently and achieve significant productivity gains. But waiting for a new technology to kick in before making other reengineering changes can be a mistake. Given the complications that inevitably arise in these situations, you may end up slowing down the reengineering effort—or bring it to a grinding halt—and pass up critical opportunities to work on improving other strategic areas of your organization.

Lesson 10: Alternate Levels of Participation

Increased participation is one of the desirable side effects of reengineering, and when it takes place, many organizations are changed irrevocably—and for the better. But it's important to remember that participation per se is not the goal of reengineering, and that alternating levels of participation may be the best strategy to ensure success (Figure 9.10).

Although it may sound reactionary, one of the most important lessons companies learn while reengineering is that applying the participative approach consistently can actually undermine the change process. That's be-

- Don't establish participation as your primary goal.

- Use participation only when it benefits the change process.

- Communicate how much participation can be expected.

FIGURE 9.10.   Lesson 10: Alternate Levels of Participation

cause some phases of reengineering benefit from participation, but others clearly do not. A thorough diagnosis, for example, can only be achieved if large numbers of people in the organization take part and contribute their input. But redesign usually works better with small teams, which are more conducive to creativity and can achieve consensus more easily.

One organization that was able to alternate levels of participation effectively during reengineering was The Principal Financial Group. When this large insurance company began to change its Individual Insurance operation, every employee in that department was required to participate in 3 days of training and QC-type activities. But when the reengineering process approached the redesign phase, the company shifted to a far more narrow participative strategy, and a small "macro modeling" team was formed to create a new organizational design.

Companies that have yet to reengineer should keep this in mind when communicating to employees about how much participation they can realistically expect. Otherwise, these companies may just raise false hopes or send out messages that must later be retracted.

Lesson 11: Work to Achieve a Sense of Closure

Any well-orchestrated reengineering effort has a clearly defined ending (Figure 9.11). That's when the organization as a whole can finally look back at what's been accomplished and ask: Have we reached the goals we set for ourselves at the beginning? Are we better off than we were before? What has this process helped us to achieve?

- Communicate reengineering results.

- Evaluate successes and failures.

- Regroup before starting another change project.

FIGURE 9.11. Lesson 11: Strive for a Sense of Closure

Too often, organizations begin their reengineering efforts with great fanfare but then allow them to trail off, never to be mentioned again. This is a serious mistake. When people are asked to participate in such a demanding change strategy, they have a right to know the results of their efforts. Otherwise, they are not likely to muster the psychological and emotional resources they will need should they be asked to reengineer again in the future.

Unlike continuous improvement, which becomes a way of life in companies that adopt it, reengineering is a transitional process that's intended to achieve specific organizational objectives. Although it's true that some companies prolong their reengineering effort by extending it from one department or business unit to another, each organization that undertakes it must take the time to absorb the changes that it made and examine its successes and failures. Working to achieve closure is one way to guarantee that this self-evaluation takes place and that the organization has a chance to regroup before taking on another major improvement project.

Lesson 12: Build an Infrastructure That Sustains Reengineering Success

One of the most critical lessons learned by organizations that reengineer is that once the process is over, steps must be taken to sustain the new level of performance that's been achieved. Implementing structural, work process, and technological changes will bring short-term improvements. But to ensure success over the long term, you also have to address the training, measurement, and compensation issues that help people adapt to the new work environment you have created (Figure 9.12).

- Emphasize training and development.

- Create measurement systems that reflect the new work environment.

- Implement reward systems that encourage a higher level of performance.

FIGURE 9.12.   Lesson 12: Build an Infrastructure to Sustain Reengineering Success

Although it's true that reengineering usually results in jobs that are more productive and satisfying, it's important to remember that these jobs are also more challenging and more complex. That's why organizations that reengineer must place an increased emphasis on training and development and promote the kinds of management styles, reward systems, and work cultures that help their people to maintain a higher level of performance and feel truly empowered in their new and more demanding roles.

Organizations that fail to build a new infrastructure to support the reengineering changes they have made run the risk of alienating their own people. It's unrealistic to think that the organizational adrenalin created during the change effort will keep people motivated and focused forever. When employees do not have the training they feel they need to do a good job, when their paycheck does not reflect their new responsibilities, or when they lack management support and cooperation in their new roles, they are likely to leave or develop a "what's in it for me?" attitude.

In the following chapter, we will examine in more detail what you can do to build the kind of infrastructure that will help you sustain your reengineering success.

10

Sustaining Reengineering: Mastering the Soft Side of Organizational Change

Although most companies that reengineer see immediate gains in quality, productivity, and customer satisfaction, there's no guarantee that these improvements will last forever. Some organizations, in fact, experience significant setbacks 2 or 3 years after reengineering, even when they have done a good job of reorganizing themselves, introducing new technologies, and redesigning jobs.

Does this mean that the reengineering approach is inherently flawed? We don't believe so. Our experience indicates that the basic principles of reengineering are sound and that their application usually results in substantial organizational benefits. But problems can arise when companies fail to do what it takes to *sustain* reengineering.

In a large bank that reengineered several business units, for example, quality and productivity breakthroughs were recorded early in every location. But there were notable variations in long-term performance among the bank's different operations. One division in particular suffered a major downturn after a couple of years when many of its most qualified people opted to leave, and most of the gains it had achieved through reengineering were quickly undone.

What happened? As in some other reengineering cases we have seen, this organization had implemented the structural, work process, and technological changes that reengineering requires—what we call the "hard stuff." But it neglected to adequately address the "soft" side of organizational change: those areas management must focus on to help people adapt to a radically changed work environment and that are critical to reengineering success over the long term (Figure 10.1).

A process and set of tools to radically and simultaneously improve:

THE "HARD" STUFF	THE "SOFT" STUFF
• organization structure	• employee empowerment
• work flows	• management style
• job design	• training processes
• physical layout	• recognition & reward systems
• technology systems	• communications & feedback
	• measurement systems

FIGURE 10.1.   Mastering Organizational Change

Reinvesting Reengineering Savings

The excitement and enthusiasm that reengineering generates is often what provides the energy people need to make it through the strain of organizational change and begin to tackle the more complex and challenging jobs that result from it. But you cannot expect people to operate on adrenalin indefinitely. Without continued training, more frequent and more effective feedback, and better recognition and reward systems, people are likely to become frustrated, burn out, or feel shortchanged.

If reengineering is so good for organizations, why does this happen? Part of the reason is that major change always inspires ambivalent feelings. True, most people find their new responsibilities more enjoyable and more satisfying—they like having more control and more customer contact—and they would prefer *not* to return to the type of job they held before their organization reengineered. But many of these same people will readily admit that their work day has become more tiring and more stressful as a result of reengineering, and that they sometimes feel nostalgic about earlier times. "I really wouldn't want to go back to the way things used to be around here," we've heard people say again and again. "But my job takes a lot more out of me now, and I worry about the business more than I ever did before."

In time, these added worries and concerns begin to take their toll on people, and the negative feelings associated with organizational change may outweigh the positive ones. That's why many organizations reach a critical point about 2 years after they have reengineered. Those that have invested some of their "savings" from reengineering into new support systems will provide the help their people need to continue performing at a higher level, and most of them will be able to sustain their reengineering success. But organizations that do not make these investments typically experience what we call the "Terrible Two's." After an initial period of improvement, indicators of organizational performance may begin to show movement in the opposite direction: morale will dip, turnover will increase, and productivity and quality gains will dissolve.

When this happens, organizations may actually end up worse off than before they reengineered. That's because their people have been transformed through reengineering into customer service or workstation "professionals," so when they leave they create a bigger gap in the organization and are far more difficult to replace. In some cases, organizations become so desperate to fill vacant positions that they end up dismantling the multiskilled jobs that they created during reengineering and revert to the less desirable assembly-line work systems they used to operate.

How to Avoid the "Terrible Two's"

In the early phases of reengineering, it's not uncommon for organizations to concentrate on making alterations to their technological and work systems, which are exciting changes to make and critical to performance improvement. But in order to achieve permanent and fundamental change through reengineering, organizations must also focus on their *human* systems. All too often, this aspect of reengineering is overlooked, with dire long-term consequences.

What can you do to avoid the "Terrible Two's"? There are three primary areas you must invest in to sustain your reengineering success:

- Continued learning.

- Measurement and feedback.

- Recognition and rewards.

Continued Learning

When companies reengineer, job requirements often change dramatically, and extensive training is necessary to help people develop new skills. In most cases, organizations meet this challenge successfully, and they do it largely through cross-training: instructing people in several, or all, the functions that need to be mastered in order to complete a work process or provide start-to-finish service for customers.

There are many different cross-training approaches, including computer-based learning, classroom instruction, and mentoring. But the most common instructional method companies use is to appoint internal experts as dedicated trainers or "coaches." These days, few organizations can rely on corporate personnel for help in cross-training, because many centralized training departments have been downsized or even eliminated. So most organizations that reengineer must draw from their own people for the talent they need to develop and implement cross-training programs.

When NationsBank reengineered its International Services Operation, for example, two of the most experienced people at its Atlanta location were designated as full-time coaches, and they developed a formal program to provide instruction in all the functions involved in a letter-of-credit transaction. The training is now conducted in two installments of 4 to 6 weeks each, and includes self-teaching manuals, case studies of sample credits, and lab work involving real letter-of-credit documents.

The Coach and the Training Package

In any given work unit, as many people as possible should be involved in planning the training program. Cross-training is more successful when those who require training are allowed to participate in designing the curriculum and setting the learning schedule. In organizations where this occurs, people are usually more receptive to training, and they develop a stronger sense of ownership over the new skills they learn.

Still, only a small group of people should be selected as trainers or coaches—those individuals who actually bear the responsibility for completing training sessions or modules (Figure 10.2). And although there are probably many people in any work unit who can do an adequate job of coaching, these positions should be reserved for managers or supervisors or for the most

---

INTERPERSONAL SKILLS

- *Expresses a desire to help others.*
- *Demonstrates a positive attitude about the job and the organization.*
- *Communicates clearly and forcefully.*
- *Is able to stimulate an interest in learning.*
- *Works effectively under pressure.*

JOB KNOWLEDGE

- *Knows how a task is properly performed.*
- *Follows departmental rules and regulations.*
- *Adheres to production and quality standards.*
- *Understands the training requirements for each job function.*

FIGURE 10.2. Guidelines for Coach Selection

experienced or knowledgeable people in the work unit. Coaches should also have strong interpersonal skills, of course, be able to work well under pressure, and know how to stimulate an interest in learning.

Coaches have five critical training responsibilities:

1. analyze and document the functions of the redesigned job.

2. prepare the training materials needed to teach the job.

3. establish training objectives and standards.

4. conduct coaching sessions with trainees.

5. provide feedback to management on trainee progress.

In most cases, the training for jobs in a reengineered organization is highly systematic and uniform for all trainees. That's because many of the tasks and procedures involved in these jobs have been exhaustively analyzed and documented during the diagnostic and redesign phases—well before the training begins—and these write-ups can be used as the basis for developing instructional materials. When no accurate documentation exists for a position, however, a "job analysis" must be prepared by a manager or coach (Figure 10.3). The objective here is to break down the job into its component

1. List the job title and the specific function being analyzed.

2. Number the tasks in completing the function, and describe the actions involved, in the order in which they take place on the job.

3. Describe clearly the objects being handled or procedures being taken.

4. Explain where and why each action is taking place.

5. Note how each action is accomplished.

6. Repeat these steps for each major job function.

FIGURE 10.3. Steps for Preparing a Job Analysis

tasks and procedures and then to present them as a series of logically related activities that complete the job.

How do you know whether your cross-training program is being conducted successfully? There are four questions you can ask that will help you determine training effectiveness. (If you answer yes to most of these questions, your cross-training efforts are probably on track.)

- Is the training being conducted on schedule—that is, are sessions being completed on the dates specified in your training timetable?

- Have production quotas been exceeded—or at least met—since the training program began?

- Have there been no or few complaints about the training from coaches or trainees?

- Do indicators of job performance show improvement (fewer errors, better quality, faster turnaround, etc.) after the training is completed?

Improving Business Knowledge and Team Skills

Some organizations that reengineer also conduct training in areas that are not strictly job-related. And although there are no research results as yet to prove that this type of training improves job performance, strong anecdotal evidence suggests that it does help to sustain reengineering and facilitates further organizational improvement.

At NationsBank, a series of classroom programs are being introduced not to teach new job skills, but solely to broaden the perspective of those who work in International Services. For example, a program has been developed to provide general information on foreign exchange trading and on how political risk affects currency fluctuations. Why devote time and energy to training that will have little direct impact on jobs? By helping people develop a better understanding of the business they work in, NationsBank firmly believes that its employees will develop a more professional attitude toward their work and become better resources for their customers and colleagues.

At AAL, too, training in areas other than functional skills became an integral part of its reengineering strategy. When the company's Insurance Product Services division reorganized into 16 self-managing teams, for example, extensive cross-training took place to help people step up to the new demands of the "bigger," multifunctional jobs created. But an advanced training program was also designed to provide people with the skills they need to sustain a more collaborative work style and to carry out management functions with decreased management support.

Developing a more participative work environment through teams often requires behavioral changes that employees cannot be expected to bring about on their own. That's why The Principal Financial Group included intensive workshops in team-building skills at the very start of the effort to reengineer its Individual Insurance operation. Even so, some of the company's managers later said that they could have done even more to help people adjust to the new team environment they created—by offering specific training in conflict resolution, for example, or by giving supervisors more support in making the transition to team leaders and coaches.

There are two types of team skills that organizations often neglect to provide adequate training for in a post-reengineering environment (Figures 10.4 and 10.5). The first are interpersonal skills, which many companies mistakenly assume will develop automatically once people are reorganized into teams. And the second are management skills, which are critical to team effectiveness, even when the teams formed are not intended to be self-managing.

Interpersonal skills training is often necessary because many people are not accustomed to working in a team environment, and they may find the constant interaction that teamwork requires uncomfortable. Besides the problems of adjusting to new routines that require them to work side by side with others,

FIGURE 10.4. Functional/Technical Skills

team members may not know how to listen to others effectively, may inadvertently demonstrate a lack of respect for the opinions of others, or may allow their personal feelings for others to interfere with how they work.

Management skills training is just as important because teams often assume supervisory responsibilities, like determining work schedules or monitoring quality and productivity indicators, after their organization has reengineered. Even teams that are not specifically set up as self-managing groups must know how to set priorities, plan projects, solve problems, and make collaborative decisions in order to work effectively. And in most cases, these are not skills that teams can learn on their own or by trial and error. On the contrary, when teams are not formally trained in the skills they need to organize their work and manage their members, they often fail to develop habits of self-reliance and, in the long run, may actually undermine organizational performance.

Whether they are designed for individuals or for teams, therefore, training efforts must continue after a change effort takes place if you want to sustain your reengineering success. That means providing the functional and technical skills people need to perform their new jobs, and giving them the interpersonal and management skills required to work effectively on teams.

Measurement and Feedback

Organizations that reengineer must also reexamine the tools they use to measure and evaluate organizational, individual, and team performance. That's

---

INTERPERSONAL SKILLS

- **Effective listening**
- **Clarifying/confirming**
- **Conflict resolution**
- **Negotiation**
- **Constructive criticism**

MANAGEMENT SKILLS

- **Time management**
- **Priority setting**
- **Decision making**
- **Problem solving**
- **Project planning**

FIGURE 10.5. Team Skills Training

because traditional measurement systems are not accurate indicators of performance in a reengineered environment, nor do they effectively promote the goals of reengineering. They are two important ways performance measurements must change once an organization has reengineered: (1) how measurements are used (Figure 10.6) and (2) the types of measurements taken.

How measurements are used. In traditional organizations, measurement is primarily a mechanism managers use for the purpose of control. When decisions are made at the top, managers need measurements to determine the impact of those decisions and how well they are being implemented by the people below. For the most part, those who are not in management view measurements negatively—as another manifestation of management dominance and control. This is understandable because these people are oftentimes exposed to measurements only during performance appraisals, when they are being fired or disciplined, or when they are being asked to achieve more demanding productivity or quality targets.

In traditional organizations:	In reengineered organizations :
• to maintain control	• to provide feedback about customer needs
• to determine the impact of management decisions	• to identify problems to assess individual and team performance
• to monitor unit or department performance	• to evaluate new job designs
• to justify corrective or disciplinary action	

FIGURE 10.6.   Reasons for Measuring

When an organization reengineers, however, many critical business decisions are delegated to empowered workers in nonmanagement positions or to customer-focused teams. And in order for these people to do their jobs, they need continuous and accurate feedback—about the quality of their work, the needs of their customers, and the effectiveness of their new job designs. In a reengineered work environment, therefore, an important shift takes place in how measurements are used. Instead of simply providing the justification for managers to take corrective or disciplinary action, measurements serve a higher purpose: to relay valuable information that people at all levels can use to solve problems, understand customers, and gauge their progress toward new organizational goals.

Which measurements are taken. The measurements that are taken in traditional organizations focus primarily on internal activities and are functionally based. Typically, each department or unit develops an elaborate set of measurements to evaluate its own performance, and these measurements flow upward on a regular basis to senior management. Despite the wealth of information collected in these organizations, however, there are relatively few measurements that reflect cross-functional results (those that do are usually financial in nature, such as gross margins, capital assets, debt, etc.), customer-related measurements are often poorly designed and haphazardly administered, and employee-related measurements (quality of work life, job motivation, etc.) are nonexistent.

Organizations that reengineer, however, must develop measurements that can track cross-functional work processes and evaluate their effectiveness (Figure 10.7). And because these processes focus primarily on "outputs" (anything that provides true value for the customer), the number of measurements that need to be taken often declines significantly and includes only key indicators of customer satisfaction (turnaround time, error rate, etc.). What measurements are *added* in a reengineered organization? Mechanisms that track job motivation and satisfaction usually need to be introduced. The reason is that when nonmanagement personnel assume greater responsibility for meeting customer needs, the importance of job-satisfaction indicators increases significantly.

Developing Team-Based and Customer-Based Measurements

When organizations reorganize into natural work units or teams, there's also a need to establish measurements that monitor—and provide a basis for improving—team performance. Not surprisingly, the most effective measurement systems are often those developed by teams themselves. In most cases, team members know best what kinds of information will help them recognize problems and identify new business opportunities. Even appraisal systems in reengineered organizations often incorporate peer reviews because team members are the best qualified to measure and evaluate each other's performance.

The sophisticated technologies that frequently accompany reengineering can also play an important role in helping teams create more effective measurement systems. In many cases, they are capable of performing instantaneous calculations (tracking the average length and frequency of customer

---

- Focus on outcomes, not activities.

- Include customer, employee, and organization (CEO) performance indicators.

- Use measures as a learning tool, not a control or "gotcha" mechanism.

- Involve teams in the development process.

- Adopt only a handful of key measures.

FIGURE 10.7. Developing Measurement Systems That Sustain Reengineering

calls, for example, or classifying types of inquiries as they come in) that provide immediate and valuable feedback teams can use to make quick adjustments in how they operate or interact with customers.

Integrating customer-based measurements into appraisals of team performance also helps to sustain reengineering success. Why? The reason is that when customers are asked directly to determine how well a team provides service or satisfies their needs, team members develop a stronger accountability to customers and are more likely to work at improving team effectiveness.

Sharing Measurements and Revising Systems

One of the most effective ways organizations can promote their reengineering goals through measurement is to communicate measurement results more widely and to revise measurement systems as improvement efforts progress (Figure 10.8).

Most organizations do a poor job of sharing measurement results across work units. But in a reengineered environment, communicating measurement results can provide a sound basis for establishing best practices among workstation professionals or teams. In one Northeast bank, for example, a formal best-practices model was developed that informed workers about the productive behaviors and techniques of others at the lowest tactical levels. At another bank, regular discussions were held among natural work units so they could compare the results of their productivity and quality efforts.

It's also important that measurement systems be continually reexamined in light of customers' changing needs and that, the closer improvement efforts approach zero-defect performance, the more they focus on specific errors rather than on percentages. There's little to be gained from knowing that accuracy improved from 99.4 to 99.6 percent within the past 2 months, for example. A far more productive approach: Count and identify the specific errors that were made, and then develop effective strategies to make sure they are not repeated.

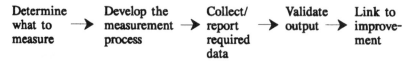

FIGURE 10.8. Developing a Performance Measurement System

Recognition and Rewards

Many companies that reengineer are willing to change just about every aspect of their organization—except how they recognize and reward people. There are two main reasons why. One is that these practices have changed little over time, and they are often viewed as sacrosanct systems that should never be violated. Another is the fear of making a serious mistake. There are no established guidelines about how to redesign these systems after reengineering, so many companies believe that if they don't do it right, the consequences could be disastrous.

Not taking any action in this area, however, is a sure way to undo the reengineering gains you have made. Whenever you redesign jobs and change the way work is performed, it only makes good sense to also change how you recognize and reward people. That's because the new work structures and challenges you create by reengineering will help maintain morale and motivation in the short term, but over time, people will begin to expect more: Many will want to be better paid for what they do and will look for different kinds of nonmonetary rewards.

In most cases, these increased expectations are understandable and justified. Although some critics might argue that the new jobs created through reengineering are simply compilations of old work functions, it's important to remember that people are held more accountable in a reengineered organization and are expected to perform at higher levels. As a result, many of them perform jobs that are much more valuable to the organization and their compensation needs to reflect that value.

Developing New Compensation Systems

Deciding how you want to change your compensation system after you reengineer will depend on factors unique to your organization: the way you have redesigned jobs, for example, your corporate culture, and what your people expect to receive. But many companies convert from a fixed compensation to some kind of variable pay system after reengineering, if only to establish a stronger connection between how people work and the results they achieve.

There are many ways you can design a compensation system to promote the concept that people should be rewarded for how much they contribute and not simply for the position they hold or how long they have been on board. Some companies introduce pay-for-knowledge programs, where compensation is based on the number of applied skills or work functions performed. Others do it through performance incentives. When specific productivity, quality, customer satisfaction, or bottom-line results are achieved, individuals receive a bonus, a share of the savings earned, or part of the new revenues generated.

Sometimes individual pay is also tied to team, division, or corporate performance, and this can be an effective way to educate people about certain business realities: the importance of cooperation and teamwork, for example, and the vagaries of the marketplace. But in these cases, the formulas for calculating compensation often become quite complicated, and unless people thoroughly understand how they are devised or play a major part in setting them up, they will not work very well. The most successful pay systems are usually the simplest ones to understand and administer.

You can drive yourself crazy trying to come up with the perfect plan for compensating your people in the new work environment you have created. But all you really have to do to develop an effective pay system is to apply the time-honored compensation principles that managers have relied on for decades. In short: Pay people what their job is worth, and make sure it's competitive.

Recognizing the Importance of Nonmonetary Rewards

The emphasis on creating just the right compensation system can also divert organizations from another issue that's critical to sustaining reengineering: providing recognition and nonmonetary rewards on a routine basis. In traditional organizations, these practices are often neglected. And even though change efforts offer new opportunities to celebrate achievements and pat people on the back, the track record in this area for organizations that reengineer is not much better.

In general, most organizations significantly underestimate the importance of providing recognition and nonmonetary rewards—even though there's plenty of evidence to support the belief that employees appreciate them even more than they do money. One insurance company, for example, devised a clever program that allowed managers to distribute a certain number of artificial coins each month to exceptional performers, and employees could cash in the coins for prizes and gifts. But over time, fewer and fewer coins were cashed in, the company found. The reason why: Employees kept the coins for display at their workstations because they valued the symbols of recognition far more than the objects they could buy with them.

Ironically, it's sometimes *because* managers become so obsessed with organizational improvement that they pass up good opportunities to recognize what their people have accomplished. In another insurance company, for example, the number of new-policy issues that could be turned around within 15 days— a key reengineering goal—increased from zero to 85 percent in just 8 months, even though head count had been significantly reduced. Yet despite this remarkable progress, the president of the organization resisted any kind of celebration, because he could only focus on the additional work that lay ahead.

There are three keys (Figure 10.9) to effective nonmonetary recognition: fairness, appropriateness, and consistency.

Whatever programs you design to acknowledge achievements, everyone should have an opportunity to participate and an equal chance to be recognized. This is often an issue with many employee-of-the-month programs, for example, because those who deal with customers or who perform highly visible jobs are frequently named as winners more often than those who work in low-skilled or back-office jobs.

Employees also know intuitively when the form of recognition you use is appropriate and when it's not, so don't feel you have to go overboard just to prove your sincerity. Sometimes the simplest demonstrations of appreciation are the most effective. For example, the president of a large Midwest firm wanted to recognize the good work of a reengineering team, so he invited it's members to a short cocktail party after work and thanked each person indi-

- Fairness

- Appropriateness

- Consistency

FIGURE 10.9. Keys to Effective Nonmonetary Recognition

vidually. Although the entire affair lasted less than an hour, it became a memorable occasion for those who attended; most had never received an invitation from the president before or had any personal contact with their organization's higher-ups.

Finally, it's important that recognition be administered consistently, as a routine part of a manager's job, and not just to acknowledge exceptional performance. Those who rarely excel in their work—but can always be relied on to show up and do a good job—should also receive some kind of recognition for their loyalty, dedication, and constant willingness to apply themselves for the benefit of their organization.

Providing Professional Growth Opportunities

Helping your people to grow and develop professionally is another important way to maintain motivation and morale and sustain reengineering success. Traditional organizations do this through promotion and career advancement. But organizations that reengineer—which are usually flatter and provide fewer opportunities for upward mobility—must develop creative alternatives (Figure 10.10).

How do you promote professional development and career growth after you have reengineered? Job rotation is one effective way to expand the possibilities for development in organizations that have a limited number of open-

---

- Job rotation.

- Ongoing business education.

- Skill and competency building.

- Apprentice–journeyman–master programs.

FIGURE 10.10. Strategies for Career Growth and Professional Development

ings at the top. By offering employees the chance to make lateral moves more frequently, you help them broaden their skill base, gain a better knowledge of the business in which they work, and add to their résumé.

Formal programs of skill building and ongoing education are other ways to satisfy employees' development needs. In NationsBank's International Services Operation, for example, everyone involved in letter-of-credit transactions takes part in career-path training to identify strengths and weaknesses and outline a plan for improving competencies. And, as stated earlier, employees also have access to classroom programs that provide a basic education in international finance should they decide to apply for other types of jobs within the corporation.

Even when organizations combine previously separate functions into "whole" jobs, they sometimes establish different skill and pay levels for the same position. This isn't simply a gimmick to convince people that they have something to work toward. In many cases, in fact, the large number of competencies that are needed to perform these jobs without assistance cannot be acquired all at once, and employees must commit themselves to an extended training program that takes place over months or even years. Job titles may even change during this learning process to reflect the skill level achieved, an approach that sometimes resembles the apprentice–journeyman–master system created by guilds during the Middle Ages to distinguish stages of professional development and still being used successfully in many European countries.

No matter what career-growth strategies you use, however, one point is clear: Even when reengineering limits the potential for advancement within your organization, it still pays to invest in the development of your people. One benefit is that it helps them to perform better in the jobs they hold now. And when their expertise exceeds your current requirements, it establishes a solid base of knowledge and skills from which you can draw whenever you need in the future.

Another benefit of continued development is that it creates a safety net for people by making them more employable, and in this age of job insecurity, they really appreciate that. One bank vice president, for example, sent all his people to a Dale Carnegie course to build their self-esteem. Although the training expense could not be justified on technical grounds, this executive knew instinctively that he did not have to calculate in dollars and cents the expected return on his investment because the value of the goodwill he created was immeasurable.

Reengineering and Continuous Improvement

Even though your company may decide to reengineer again in the future, you need to establish an organizational infrastructure in the meantime to support your people in their new work environment and give them the tools they need to meet new and more demanding challenges. The three techniques outlined in this chapter will help you accomplish this. They provide an integrated strategy you can use to sustain your reengineering gains and capitalize on the productivity and quality improvements you have made.

Just as important, these techniques can help you build a solid foundation for continuous improvement.

Many organizations assume that once they reengineer, productivity and quality improvement will automatically become a way of life. But that doesn't happen unless you meet the prerequisites to long-term improvement: training your people in the right skills, developing effective measurement systems, and giving appropriate recognition and rewards. When you do, your people become motivated not only to continue to work, but also to *improve* their work.

Although it's true that reengineering can help realize dramatic breakthroughs from time to time, the significant resources involved make this a change strategy that you can realistically implement only occasionally. Other steps must be taken if you want to continue to improve on a permanent basis. What you do to sustain reengineering is often the key to continuous improvement and the best way to help your organization achieve long-term success.

Recommended Reading

Attenello, Dennis. "Re-engineering to Achieve Breakthrough Results." *TMA Journal* (March/April 1995): pp. 6–11.

Baloff, Nicholas, and Elizabeth Doherty. "Potential Pitfalls in Employee Participation." *Organizational Dynamics* (Winter 1989): pp. 51–62.

Bowen, David E., and Edward E. Lawler III. "The Empowerment of Service Workers: What, Why, How and When." *Sloan Management Review* (Spring 1992): pp. 31–39.

Clarke, J. Barry, Eileen F. Mahoney, and Susan E. Robishaw. "New England Telephone Opens Lines to Change and Hears About It from Satisfied Customers." *National Productivity Review* (Winter 1992/93): pp. 73–82.

Dalziel, Murray M., and Stephen C. Schoonover. *Changing Ways: A Practical Tool for Implementing Change Within Organizations.* New York: AMACOM, 1988.

Davenport, Thomas H. *Process Innovation: Reengineering Work through Information Technology.* Boston: Harvard Business School Press, 1993.

Ford, Robert N. *Motivation Through the Work Itself.* New York: AMACOM, 1969.

Hackman, J. Richard. "The Psychology of Self-Management in Organizations" in *Psychology and Work: Productivity, Change, and Employment.* New York: American Psychological Association, 1986, pp. 85–136.

Hackman, J. Richard, Greg Oldham, Robert Janson, and Kenneth Purdy. "A New Strategy for Job Enrichment." *California Management Review* (Summer 1975): pp. 57–71.

Hall, Gene, Jim Rosenthal, and Judy Wade. "How to Make Reengineering Really Work." *Harvard Business Review* (November/December 1993): pp. 119–131.

Hammer, Michael, and James Champy. *Reengineering the Corporation: A Manifesto for Business Revolution.* New York: HarperBusiness, 1993.

Harbour, Jerry L. *The Process Reengineering Workbook: Practical Steps to Working Faster and Smarter Through Process Improvement.* White Plains, NY: Quality Resources, 1994.

Harrington-Mackin, Deborah. *The Team Building Tool Kit: Tips, Tactics, and Rules for Effective Workplace Teams.* New York: AMACOM, 1994.

Huff, Sid L. "Reengineering the Business." *You and the Computer* (Winter 1992).

Janson, Robert. "Achieving Service Excellence in the Financial Services Industry." *National Productivity Review* (Spring 1989).

Janson, Robert. "Eight Steps Toward Companywide Change." *Executive Excellence* (May 1988).

Janson, Robert. "Reengineering: Transforming Organizations in the Decade of the Customer." *National Productivity Review* (Winter 1992/93): pp. 45–53.

Janson, Robert, and Richard L. Gunderson. "The Team Approach to Company-wide Change." *National Productivity Review* (Winter 1990/91): pp. 35–43.

Kaplan, Robert B., and Laura Murdock. "Core Process Redesign." *The McKinsey Quarterly,* 2 (1991): pp. 27–43.

Kilmann, Ralph. *Managing Beyond the Quick Fix: A Completely Integrated Program for Creating and Maintaining Organizational Success.* San Francisco: Jossey-Bass, 1989.

Matteis, Richard J. "The New Back Office Focuses on Customer Service." *Harvard Business Review* (March/April 1979): pp. 146–159.

Meyer, Christopher. "How the Right Measures Help Teams Excel." *Harvard Business Review* (May/June 1994): pp. 96–103.

Mohrman, Allan M., et al. *Large-Scale Organizational Change.* San Francisco: Jossey-Bass, 1989.

Ostroff, Frank, and Douglas Smith. "The Horizontal Organization." *The McKinsey Quarterly,* 1 (1992): pp. 148–168.

Parry, Scott B. *From Managing to Empowering: An Action Guide to Developing Winning Facilitation Skills.* White Plains, NY: Quality Resources, 1994.

Potts, Mark, and Peter Behr. *The Leading Edge: CEOs Who Turned Their Companies Around—What They Did and How They Did It.* New York: McGraw-Hill, 1987.

Pugh, Stuart. *Total Design: Integrated Methods for Successful Product Engineering.* Reading, MA: Addison-Wesley, 1991.

Rohm, Charles. "The Principal Insures a Better Future Through Reengineering." *National Productivity Review* (Winter 1992/93): pp. 55–64.

Ryan, Alan J. "Cigna Re-engineers Itself." *Computerworld* 25(27) (July 9, 1991): pp. 79–81.

Spadaford, Joseph. "Reengineering Commercial Loan Services at First Chicago." *National Productivity Review* (Winter 1992/93): pp. 65–72.

Spector, Bert A. "From Bogged Down to Fired Up: Inspiring Organizational Change." *Sloan Management Review* (Summer 1989): pp. 29–35.

Stewart, Thomas A. "Reengineering: The Hot New Managing Tool." *Fortune* (August 23, 1993): pp. 40–8.

Talwar, Rohit. "Business Re-engineering—a Strategy-Driven Approach." *Long Range Planning*, 26 (December 1993): pp. 22–40.

Tichy, Noel M., and Mary Anne Devanna. *The Transformational Leader.* New York: John Wiley, 1986.

Truell, George F. *Employee Involvement: A Guidebook for Managers.* Buffalo: PAT Publications, 1991.

Uzzi, John. "Management Must Motivate Employees." *Servicing Management*, 5(12) (August 1994).

Weisbord, Marvin. *Productive Workplaces: Organizing and Managing for Dignity, Meaning, and Community.* San Francisco: Jossey-Bass, 1987.

Wellins, Richard S., William C. Byham, and Jeanne M. Wilson. *Empowered Teams: Creating Self-directed Work Groups That Improve Quality, Productivity, and Participation.* San Francisco: Jossey-Bass, 1991.

Wilkins, Alan L. *Developing Corporate Character: How to Successfully Change an Organization Without Destroying It.* San Francisco: Jossey-Bass, 1989.

Index